THE ROYAL HORTICULTURAL SOCIETY
PRACTICAL GUIDES

HERB
GARDENS

THE ROYAL HORTICULTURAL SOCIETY
PRACTICAL GUIDES

HERB
GARDENS

RICHARD ROSENFELD

DORLING KINDERSLEY
LONDON • NEW YORK • SYDNEY • MOSCOW
www.dk.com

A DORLING KINDERSLEY BOOK
www.dk.com

PROJECT EDITOR Cangy Venables
ART EDITOR Margherita Gianni

SERIES EDITOR Pamela Brown
SERIES ART EDITOR Stephen Josland

MANAGING EDITOR Louise Abbott
MANAGING ART EDITOR Lee Griffiths

DTP DESIGNER Matthew Greenfield

PRODUCTION MANAGER Patricia Harrington

First published in Great Britain in 1999
by Dorling Kindersley Limited,
9 Henrietta Street, London WC2E 8PS

A CIP catalogue for this book is available from the British Library.
ISBN 0 7513 06916

Reproduced by Colourpath, London
Printed and bound by Star Standard Industries, Singapore

CONTENTS

HERBS IN THE GARDEN

WHAT IS A HERB?

THE WORD "HERB" has been used for centuries to describe plants with medicinal, culinary and aromatic properties, many linked with spiritual well-being and sacred rites. No working kitchen garden was complete without a scattering of favourites such as parsley and thyme, and the simplicity of cottage-style herbs is still valued in informal plantings. But it is the formal, patterned herb gardens of the past that are popular today – features that are not only useful, but rich with historical associations and of lasting ornamental value, too.

HOW HERB GARDENS DEVELOPED

The making of special gardens in which herbs are grown and displayed has a long history. Obviously, such gardens gathered useful plants together for convenience, but there is much more of a tradition of making decorative features out of these plantings than, say, for vegetables.

From the earliest records, herbs have been associated with religion. In ancient Persia, the enclosed garden filled with scented and healing plants provided a sanctuary or "paradise" for meditation. Stylistically, European monastic gardens followed the Eastern tradition – peaceful retreats sheltered from the outside world, in which narrow pathways divided small beds that were not just decorative, but practical: powerful medicinal herbs could be grown separately, with no likelihood of confusion when gathered by novices.

RESTFUL FORMALITY
In this scene from an ancient Eastern garden, where plants each had their own separate areas, the origins of the formal garden style, with patterned, edged beds, can be seen.

◄ HERBS AS GARDEN PLANTS
Herbs can be used in mixed plantings (here, sage with apples, roses and geraniums) but special herb gardens have great appeal.

HERB GARDENS FOR STUDY

The study of plants and their medicinal uses spread from religious to scholarly institutions, who adopted the form of the patterned herb garden, with herbs in discrete beds, as a way of cultivating and displaying plants for ease of study by botanists, doctors and artists. The first of these "physic gardens" recorded in detail was created in Italy at the University of Padua in 1545, followed by others at Leyden, Holland, in 1587 and Oxford in 1621. By the end of the 17th century there were physic gardens throughout Europe.

As colonial explorers and plant-hunters brought back different species, more and more herbs from other cultures were added to the gardens' ever-expanding collections. Settlers took plants and gardening traditions with them, too: the first botanical garden in North America was created near Philadelphia in 1728, and traditional European-style herb gardens can still also be seen in Canada, Australia, New Zealand and South Africa.

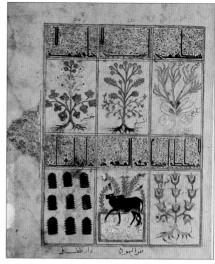

▲ EARLY EASTERN REPRESENTATION
This illustration from an early Arabic text shows an emphasis on botanical detail, marking a new appreciation of herbs as garden plants.

▼ GARDEN OF PRIVACY
This gorgeously patterned, 17th-century walled garden has walkways between the beds.

HERBS IN PRIVATE GARDENS

Meanwhile, however, cottage gardeners continued to grow herbs informally amongst ornamental plants much as they always had, both for their decorative qualities and to add to the cooking pot. But the formal, well-tended herb gardens of the institutions had enormous snob appeal for rich, private landowners, being just the sort of labour-intensive feature that displayed obvious wealth and, as a bonus, reflected the owner's scholarly and aesthetic

> Today, herb gardening is undergoing a great revival

appreciation of "nature". Soon herbs, formerly humble plants of the kitchen garden, were being grown prominently in elaborate parterres, potagers and knot gardens in palaces, stately homes and country seats.

HERB GARDENING TODAY

The great revival of interest in herb gardening today combines elements from the scholarly, grand and cottage traditions. In the East, herb growing has largely remained functional, for medicinal purposes; in their own gardens, the Chinese and Japanese do not regard herbs as ornamentals. But in the West, it is their decorative appeal and culinary uses that are more appreciated, and herbs can be seen growing everywhere from windowsills to herbaceous borders, used simply as ornamental plants or, in today's smaller gardens, in greatly scaled-down versions of the more formal, patterned beds. There are specialist nurseries where you might find up to 18 varieties of basil and 50 lavenders and, in the wake of such popularity, even the more obscure herbs, such as skirret and fleabane, are making a comeback.

MODERN HERB GARDEN
Modern herb gardens often echo the past, as with this decorative sundial centrepiece.

Why Grow Herbs?

Herbs are versatile plants. They will grow happily in most environments, they suit small gardens well, and can be used in all sorts of ways. You may grow them for cooking or simple herbal remedies, or to use in crafts and hobbies: for making pot-pourris and sachets for scenting clothes and bedlinen, even for dyeing. Alternatively, you could design a herb garden feature simply to provide a peaceful retreat, filled with soft colours and soothing aromas.

Planting with Herbs

The attraction of herbs lies to a large extent in their uses, historical associations and fragrance. The sheer number of different herbs now available, however, makes them increasingly valuable as ornamental plants. Flowers can be vivid – the red of bergamot and the oranges and yellows of pot marigolds, for example – and foliage attractive: the silver-grey of lavender, the dusky tones of purple sage and bright splash of golden marjoram.

Herbs lend themselves to both formal and informal use. Bear in mind that formal patterns need to be kept in order; plants must be carefully chosen and kept neat and bushy with regular care and clipping. But many herbs are large, wild flowering plants with a naturally loose, spreading habit; these can be allowed to grow and self-seed at will for a more informal effect.

FORMAL HERB FEATURE
This purely decorative feature uses differently coloured gravels to enhance a living pattern made of clipped herb plants.

HERBS IN POTS
Herbs with tough, wiry stems that grow naturally in poor or hot, dry soil are perfect for pots. Here (from left), bay, santolina, rosemary and thymes form an attractive, aromatic group. Softer-stemmed plants such as the parsley (second from left) can be pot-grown, but need regular watering.

GROWING HERBS FOR USE

Today, most gardeners grow herbs to pick chiefly for their culinary uses (*see pp.12–13*), and for this, a specially-made herb garden or bed is ideal, keeping all the plants needed together and readily accessible. Many herbs grow well in containers (*pp.46–51*); these may be placed on steps, windowsills or conveniently by the kitchen door. The regular harvesting of the herbs helps keep them in check, preventing them from swamping their neighbours or spoiling a design.

> Regular harvesting of herbs helps keep them shapely and in check

The medicinal purposes of herbs should be treated with respect and caution, but many can be grown in small herb gardens for occasional use in simple, therapeutic ways (*see pp.16–17*), such as in teas and infusions. Herbs grown for crafts and hobbies (*see pp.18–20*) may need to be grown in greater quantity, so you should plan to allocate more room for them, perhaps giving individual plants or types of plants beds of their own.

▲ KITCHEN HERB GARDEN
Narrow beds of culinary herbs no more than a metre across, with paths alongside, make access for tending and harvesting easy.

▼ HERBS IN INFORMAL PLANTINGS
Untamed herbs grown in the ornamental border create a lovely, naturalistic effect, with the added attraction of encouraging wildlife.

CULINARY HERBS

CULINARY HERBS, mostly easy to grow, can enhance the flavour of any dish. Whatever size your garden, there will be room to generate plenty of wonderful tastes. The range of kitchen herbs includes shrubs, perennials and annuals that may be creeping, clump-forming, towering or even climbing in habit; enough, in a small garden, to create a completely edible landscape.

A KITCHEN HERB GARDEN

A herb garden designed with healing plants to provide a quiet retreat might well be best situated in an out-of-the-way part of the garden, but if you plan to use the herbs as a kitchen resource, it's more practical either to incorporate them into the kitchen garden, if you have one, or to grow them together near the house. Here, your herb bed will probably be on show by a door or visible from windows, so it makes sense to design it as an attractive feature that will not look bare and gloomy in winter. Hard landscaping materials can be a real bonus: a chequerboard design (*see pp.28–32*) set into a patio, for example, has year-round structural appeal, as do groups of interesting containers (*see pp.34–39*) or brick-patterned beds (*see pp.46–51*). But there are shrubby, evergreen kitchen herbs that can add structure to a planting: rosemary, sages and thymes, for example (though they do look a little scruffy after a cold winter). For elegant good looks and usefulness year-round, there is little to beat a carefully shaped bay tree; not cheap to buy, but a lasting investment. If you don't mind losing the outlines of your beds in winter, there are lots of herbaceous culinary herbs that make beautiful edging: rows of chives allowed to flower, for example, or emerald ribbons of curly parsley.

HERBS IN THE BORDER
Culinary herbs that you do not use often can be scattered among plantings of ornamentals: here, feathery dill and large-leaved lovage add height with foxgloves, while golden marjoram weaves through santolina. Grow them in groups or drifts, so that any harvesting does not spoil the planting.

COLOURS AND TEXTURES

Your choice of herbs to fill kitchen beds will probably be guided more by their flavours (*see overleaf*) than by looks, and you may find that foliage plants with relatively small flowers predominate. With some herbs, too, such as rocket and basil, flowerheads need removing regularly if the

> Remove flowerheads from basil and rocket to intensify the flavour

leaves are to retain their flavour (this can be surprisingly time-consuming). But even using foliage it is possible to ring colour changes – with, for example, silver sage or purple-leaved basil. You could also allot a little space to some herbs with edible flowers; a small wigwam of canes covered with climbing nasturtiums would make a striking centrepiece for a symmetrical culinary herb garden.

▲ A FEAST OF FOLIAGE
Nasturtiums and pot marigolds, which can be used in salads, will brighten up a group of leafy kitchen herbs. Here, mints grown in pots to restrain them can be moved to fill gaps.

▼ FLOWERING FREELY
Grow plenty of chives (here with fennel and Good King Henry) so that you can allow some to develop their drumstick flowerheads.

GROWING HERBS FOR THE KITCHEN

IF YOU ARE USED to cooking with herbs, you will probably have some ideas about what you want to grow in a culinary herb garden. But if you are a new cook (and particularly if you are a new gardener too), it's not easy to know which will be the most useful herbs, how many plants you should buy, and – with so many different types to choose from – which are actually the culinary herbs, and which are the more ornamental, less flavoursome varieties.

HOW MUCH SPACE?

You can make a kitchen herb "survival kit" in a container no larger than a shoebox (*see below*), but you must be prepared to tend, water, trim and even replace plants frequently: many different plants packed together like this will not thrive for long, although they do make a more lasting resource than the small pots of living herbs available at supermarkets. With a small herb garden, you can grow a whole range of herbs happily together, provided that you take measures to restrain inveterate spreaders like mints and marjorams. Don't waste space, either, in a small herb garden on a lot of large plants that you will only

use rarely; they can be accommodated instead in a border, if attractive, or in a corner of a vegetable plot.

WHICH HERBS TO CHOOSE?

Herbs are so popular these days that it is now usual to see herb plants labelled with common names at garden centres, so you don't need to know their Latin names, but even so, you need to choose carefully – eau-de-cologne mint may be a prettier plant than common mint, but it will give new potatoes a very peculiar flavour.

Faced with a wide range of herb plants attractively displayed, it's tempting to fill a basket with a dozen small specimens, all

MINI KITCHEN GARDEN
A windowsill could accommodate this wire basket, lined with moss, then pierced polythene, and filled with compost, but you must tend and water the plants regularly. Always plant mints in their pots to prevent them overwhelming other plants. At the end of the summer, it is best to plant all of the hardy herbs out in the garden.

If space is limited, be ruthless and reserve your herb garden for kitchen favourites (below). Borage (left) may be pretty, but you probably won't use it that often: a large plant, it is better sited where there is more room for it.

of different kinds. However, not only will this make your herb garden look bitty, but it will take an age for them to grow large enough to be useful: one recipe calling for a

> Always grow twice as much parsley as you think you need

handful of chervil, and you could demolish an entire plant. Three or four plants each of a few real kitchen standbys soon make attractive and productive clumps.

How Many Plants?

With some herb flavours, less is definitely more, but fresh, leafy summer herbs like coriander are best by the bunchful. As a general rule, and perhaps a frustrating one for gardeners less confident of their skills, the more robust and long-lived the plant, the less you need to use of it. A single

rosemary bush, for example, needs virtually no looking after and can supply several kitchens with sprigs for years, but if your dishes regularly call for great handfuls of parsley and basil, bought plants will last no time at all and you will have to consider growing your own plants from seed (*see p.56*), sowing not just once but several times during the spring and summer to keep plants coming.

CLASSIC COMBINATIONS

Standby herbs for different dishes include:

Fish Bay, chervil, dill, fennel, lovage, parsley, sorrel, sweet cicely, winter savory.

Beef Bay, rosemary, tarragon, thyme.

Chicken Chervil, chives, coriander, fennel, parsley, tarragon.

Pork Basil, coriander, fennel, pot marigold, marjoram, parsley, sorrel, thyme.

Lamb Coriander, oregano, parsley, rosemary.

Eggs Basil, chervil, chives, coriander, dill, fennel, summer savory, sorrel, tarragon, thyme.

MEDICINAL HERBS

PLANTS WERE THE FIRST MEDICINES available, and have played an important role in our well-being ever since. When different cultures started recording knowledge they had gained, the healing potential of herbs was a key subject. Nearly 1,000 years before the West even had a printing press, the Chinese produced their *Canon*, listing over 800 medicinal herbs and their uses.

HERBS WITH HEALING POWERS

In any country, it takes years of training to become a qualified herbalist, but, in cultures where herbal medicine is not now mainstream, we have largely forgotten that there was a time when everyone would instinctively seek out certain plants as simple remedies. Today, we are far more likely to reach for the medicine cabinet for relief from pain or discomfort, although many undoubtedly effective folk remedies do persist – applying a dock leaf to nettle-stings, for example. Western medical science has, however, long acknowledged a debt to the herbal tradition – while our forebears chewed willow bark to alleviate headaches, we might now take aspirin, whose active ingredient, salicylic acid, was

> Modern medical science has long acknowledged its debt to plants

first isolated in willow (*Salix*). While it can be interesting to experiment on a small scale with simple, safe remedies for some

► CLARY SAGE
The Latin name,
Salvia, *for this healing herb stems from the word for "safe".*

▼ ESSENCES AND OILS
The benefits of evening primrose oil are widely recognized.

TWO FOR TEA
*Fresh sprigs of mint
or chamomile* (left)
*make soothing teas,
steeped in boiling
water. Let mint tea
cool, adding a little
honey if desired,
for a refreshing
summer drink.*

mild discomforts (*see below*) it is essential not to dabble further into herbal medicine without guidance or the help of an authoritative book. What you can do, however, without preparing or taking any remedy at all, is simply to benefit from the therapeutic effects of making and tending a garden planted with herbs that have healing properties and associations. The attractions of, say, a daily glass of borage infusion might soon begin to pall, but you will gain lasting enjoyment from a herb garden full of pretty plants with relaxing or uplifting aromas: a place to unwind and let tensions ease away. The scents, tactile foliage, quiet orderliness of the beds and their air of seclusion have made this type of "healing" herb garden increasingly popular; indeed, for many hospitals they are now *de rigueur*, as an outdoor sunroom in which convalescent patients can benefit from the restorative power of plants.

SOME SIMPLE REMEDIES	METHOD
Teas: mint to settle the stomach; chamomile or vervain to soothe; lemon balm to uplift.	Immerse 75g of fresh herbs (or 30g of dried herbs) in 500ml of near-boiling water.
Infusions: borage and lavender to fight colds; yarrow to relieve catarrh; lemon balm to relieve flatulence.	Make as for tea; leave to cool and use as a specific remedy or as an invigorating drink. It is best to make infusions fresh each day.
Ointments: arnica or comfrey to quell bruising; chamomile or St John's wort to alleviate minor skin conditions.	Heat 60g of dried herbs in 500g petroleum jelly over boiling water for about 2 hours. While still hot, strain into a jar. Leave to cool.
Inhalations: borage and lavender to fight colds; yarrow to relieve catarrh.	Add 500ml of an infusion (*above*) to a basin of hot water and inhale steam under a towel.
Bath relaxant or tonic: chamomile or vervain as a relaxant; comfrey, pot marigold, nettle or yarrow as a restorative tonic.	Fill a muslin bag with fresh or dried herbs. Fasten neck and hang around hot water tap so that water soaks it. Squeeze juice into bath.

HERBS FOR THE HOME

O THER TRADITIONAL USES for herbs are preserved in many crafts and hobbies. Dried, they can be enjoyed in lasting ways around the home – in bowls of pot-pourri, as garlands, wreaths and in dried-flower arrangements. They can scent pillows and sachets, candles and writing paper, and form the basis for many traditional dyes (*see overleaf*). Remember that the more serious you become about your hobby, the more space you will need to allocate to plants.

POT-POURRIS AND WREATHS

Easy to make, a pot-pourri consists of a mix of dried flowers and scented foliage, sometimes with seedheads and dried bark. Chemists and craft shops stock special fixatives, complete with instructions, which lock in the aromas for longer – powdered orris root or gum benzoin are the most common. You can also buy essential oils to boost or revive scents. Use these frugally, however, since they easily dominate more subtle aromas.

For drying (*see p.58*), herb leaves should be picked early, the moment the dew has evaporated, and flowers as they open. You might choose a theme for a pot-pourri: a herb leaf mix, or a flower, lemon or even wild garden mix. For a herb leaf pot-pourri try lemon balm, marjoram, mint, rosemary, sage and thyme. To a flower mix made bright with bergamot and yarrow, add other scented garden flowers, such as roses and philadelphus. For spicy winter scents, try adding fresh, ground cardamom, cloves, coriander or fennel seed, and dried lemon, lime or orange peel. Cover for 4–6 weeks

> ## Pick herbs early in the morning, as soon as the dew is dry

before using, to allow time for the scents to merge and intensify. Another traditional way of displaying herbs is in a wreath. Roll up a rectangle of chicken wire and join the ends to form a ring frame, then weave in

SUMMER SCENTS
Bags of dried lavender are a favourite way of keeping linen fresh, bringing memories of summer scents all year round. This lavender, with its zany bracts, is Lavandula stoechas, *or French lavender; it needs a sheltered spot.*

fresh thyme, sage, lavender and rosemary with florist's moss. Leave to dry in a warm, airy place. Simple bunches of dried herbs arranged in a basket also look decorative.

MORE HERB IDEAS

For the bedroom, take a few handfuls of pot-pourri and sew them inside small, decorative covers to put beside pillows. You could even make aromatic sachets to hang in the car. Scented candles can be made by adding dried herbs just before the mould stage. You can also make scented notepaper by scattering layers of dried herbs between the sheets in a box.

Even if you are not the least bit "crafty", herbs can enhance the home. Simple but stylish, fresh bunches of leafy and flowering herbs make lovely table decorations for summer parties and meals, with a home-made look that bought flowers cannot match. A deft touch for a dinner party is to put small bowls of fresh, edible herbs – say, parsley, basil and rocket – on the table, allowing guests to help themselves.

▲ FRAGRANCE IN THE HOME
Many scented plants, including meadowsweet, above, were once used as "strewing herbs", scattered on bare floors to cover other, less attractive smells.

▼ BOLD AND BEAUTIFUL
For large bowls, make bold pot-pourris with whole dried flowerheads, to avoid the shredded, "nose-bag" look; here yarrow and pot marigolds contribute to a sunny theme.

WOAD

COMFREY

CONTRASTING COLOURS
Yellow-flowered woad has been
produce a blue colour for centuries, while
comfrey will yield a sunny yellow dye.

DYEING WITH HERBS

Dyeing is tricky but fun, and you need a room where splashes will not be a problem. Note, too, that each batch of dye solution will produce a slightly different colour. If dyeing natural wool, you need to scour it first by washing thoroughly or soaking for a few hours to remove any oil. The dye is made in advance; the process usually involves steeping herbs in a bowl of water

The intensity of dye colours depends on the quantity of the herb used

for eight hours, before simmering them for two more. Cool the solution, remove the herbs, add the garment, and simmer again for an hour. Then simmer the garment in a commercial mordant solution that will fix the colour, following the instructions for quantities and timing. Different mordants can produce different colours from the same plant (*see below*). When the solution has again cooled, remove the garment with tongs and rinse it until the water is clear.

COLOURS FROM HERB DYES

HERB	PART USED	MORDANT	COLOUR
Agrimony	Flowering tops	Alum	Butter yellow
Comfrey	Whole plant	Alum	Yellow
Chamomile	Flowers	Alum, cream of tartar	Bright yellow
Meadowsweet	Roots	Alum	Black
Nettles	Whole plant	Alum, cream of tartar, pinch of ferrous sulphate	Greenish-grey
Nettles	Whole plant	Copper sulphate	Soft grey-green
Parsley	Whole plant	Alum	Cream
Pot marigolds	Petals	Alum, cream of tartar	Pale yellow
Safflower	Flowers	Alum	Yellow and tan
St John's wort	Flowers	Alum	Cream
Sorrel	Whole plant	Alum	Greyish-yellow
Sorrel	Roots	Alum	Soft pink
Tansy	Flowering tops	Alum	Mustard yellow
Woad	Leaves	Sodium dithionite, ammonia	Blue

MAKING A HERB GARDEN

KNOT GARDENS P.23

A SPECIALLY DESIGNED HERB GARDEN is an ideal way to grow and display plants. The projects shown here are all on a small scale, easy to lay out, build and plant in no more than a weekend, but you can adjust the dimensions to suit your own needs: a builder's merchant should be able to advise on increasing quantities of materials, if necessary. The time taken for the feature to mature might, however, influence your choice: a formal garden that uses plants as edging (*see pp.22–27*) will take a few years to look at its best, while paving- or brick-surrounded beds (*see pp.28–39*) will fill out within a season, and a pretty container packed with young plants (*see pp.46–51*)

BRICK WHEEL P.35

can look splendid almost immediately. There is no "best" time of year to start making a herb garden, although spring provides both clement conditions for working and gives young plants the whole season in which to grow. Similarly, there is no "best" site; although most herbs do prefer a sunny position, it is

SCREE GARDEN P.41

possible to gather together a selection of plants that thrive in shade. The majority are unfussy about soil, although you might need to improve drainage (*see p.52*), particularly if you want to grow plants native to Mediterranean regions: for these, a purpose-made gravel or scree garden (*see pp.40–45*) is ideal.

HERB CASCADE P.49

FORMAL HERB GARDENS

COMPACT HERBS ARE IDEALLY SUITED to formal features. Their extensive range of leaf shapes and colours can be used both to create distinct geometrical patterns, and to infill large squares and loops of clipped low edging. Knot gardens and parterres provide popular design templates, using hedging herbs to create compartments within which any number and type of herbs can be contained. The design may be simple or complex, much of its character derived from the type of plants used and the regularity with which edging is clipped.

A SIMPLE BOX-EDGED GARDEN

This basic pattern covers an area about 3.3×3.3m, and comprises four beds divided by paths. Below the paths and edging, a sheet of polyester geotextile suppresses weeds and conserves soil moisture. Allow two days to complete the project.

HEDGING TIPS
• Buy all edging plants from the same nursery – or grow your own for economy – so they are of a uniform standard.
• Trim box plants in late spring and late summer; never when frost is likely.
• When clipping, a sheet of polythene laid alongside the hedge will collect trimmings.

COMPLETED GARDEN
Allow three to five years for box to mature, during which time regular trimming is essential to perfect its shape.

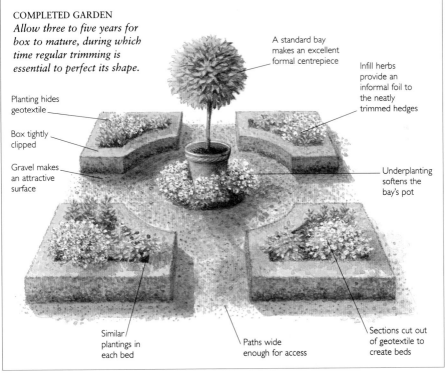

A standard bay makes an excellent formal centrepiece

Infill herbs provide an informal foil to the neatly trimmed hedges

Planting hides geotextile

Box tightly clipped

Gravel makes an attractive surface

Underplanting softens the bay's pot

Similar plantings in each bed

Paths wide enough for access

Sections cut out of geotextile to create beds

◀ GRAND STYLE *Chives and santolina (cotton lavender) alternate as infilling between box hedges.*

YOU NEED:

TOOLS
- Club hammer
- Tape measure
- Builder's square
- Scissors
- Fork • Spade
- Trowel
- Permanent marker pen
- Wire-cutters

MATERIALS
- Marker pegs
- String
- 3.5 × 3.5m sheet of geotextile
- Roll of galvanized wire
- 100kg gravel

WORKING PLAN

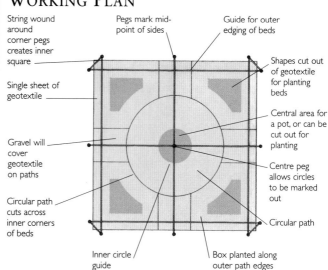

String wound around corner pegs creates inner square

Pegs mark mid-point of sides

Guide for outer edging of beds

Single sheet of geotextile

Shapes cut out of geotextile for planting beds

Gravel will cover geotextile on paths

Central area for a pot, or can be cut out for planting

Circular path cuts across inner corners of beds

Centre peg allows circles to be marked out

Circular path

Inner circle guide

Box planted along outer path edges

MARKING OUT AND LAYING GEOTEXTILE

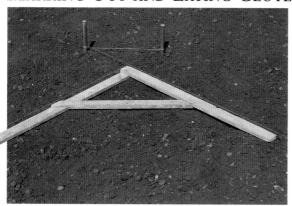

1 **Mark out** a perfect square for the outer box edging (sheets of geotextile may not be completely true and make unreliable guides). Lay a builder's square on the ground where you want the "first" corner, and hammer pegs 15cm beyond each edge. Wind string around them to cross as shown at the square's tip. Measure 3.2m along the string, place the square and repeat, then take the string on until all four sides are formed.

2 **Ease the sheet of** geotextile in under the string square, pulling it flat and trimming if necessary. Leave a generous overlap beyond the guide – the surplus fabric will give the roots of the young box plants protection on the outer edge of the garden, and can be concealed with soil or a turf, gravel or paved surround.

FINDING THE CENTRE AND SECURING FABRIC

1 **To find the centre of** the site you need to find the mid-point of each side. With these dimensions, it will be 1.6m from the corner made by the crossing string. Hammer a peg into the ground to mark the position.

2 **Run lengths of string** between the pairs of opposite pegs so that they form a cross. The point at which the lines meet is the centre of the square. Insert a peg at this point, piercing the material first (*see below*).

3 **Secure the fabric** at approximately 30cm intervals with lengths of wire bent into hoops. Always use the end of the wire or a bradawl to pierce holes in the geotextile before hammering hooks or pegs through it. This puts less strain on the material, and prevents it from bunching up.

MARKING OUT THE PATHS

1 **To mark the central** circular path, draw two circles around the central peg, using a length of string tied to it. Make knots at 30cm and 90cm from the peg, hold the marker pen against the knots and inscribe the circles.

2 **Mark out the** four paths by measuring 30cm either side of the string guides that cross at the centre. Use a permanent marker and the builder's square to ensure that the lines are straight and right-angles are true.

CUTTING AWAY FABRIC AND PLANTING

1 Cut away the geotextile for the four areas to be planted with infill herbs, leaving a 10cm overlap of fabric within the beds, and from the central disc if desired. Peg the fabric down at intervals with wire hooks, as before.

2 Position the box plants around the path edges and perimeter, spacing them approximately 8cm apart. Mark their positions and cut crosses in the fabric. Opening the sides of the crosses, make holes and plant the box, then water well.

PLANTS AND GEOTEXTILE

Purpose-made garden geotextiles have a huge advantage over other more economical materials used to suppress weeds, such as black polythene, because they allow water through into the soil, while still minimizing its loss the other way – from the soil into the atmosphere. They are available in rolls of various widths in most garden centres; lengths can be overlapped over large areas.

3 Tread along the path areas to compact the soil, remove the string, and spread a 1cm layer of gravel (or pea shingle or bark chippings) on the paths and around the box. As well as hiding the geotextile, it will keep the roots of the box plants cool.

4 Arrange the infill herbs in their positions, having first watered each plant thoroughly. Then remove them from their pots and plant. During the dry season, water regularly until the knot garden is established.

HERBS USED

EDGING
100 × Box

INFILLING
8 × Gingermint
12 × Golden feverfew
16 × Variegated lemon balm

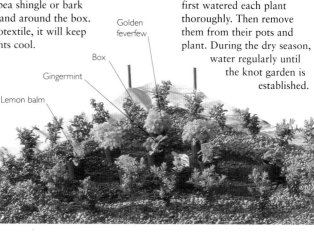

Golden feverfew

Box

Gingermint

Lemon balm

BLOCKS OF COLOUR

Most people fill in formally edged beds with a variety of plants, but for real impact, group dense, low plants of the same type closely to form striking patchwork designs. With open-knot designs *(illustrated below)* the colour of the path material can also play a part. A closed-knot design *(see photograph, below right)* has broader, interlaced hedges and beds, with no room for paths; closed knots are very difficult to tend but do look superb.

CREATING SINGLE BLOCKS OF COLOUR

SQUARED UP
Purple and green-leaved basil provide the beds' colour theme, while blue-flowered hyssop draws the eye to the centre of this design.

CROSSING PATHS
Here, the contrast between blocks of purple (lavender) and yellowy-gold (santolina in flower) produces a wonderfully vibrant effect.

TEXTURED TRIANGLES
Each section in this design could be filled with a variety of thymes and sages, creating an elegant assortment of green, gold and purple.

HERBS FOR KNOT GARDENS

FOR EDGING
These plants have an upright habit and suit regular clipping:
Box
Curry plant
Hyssop
Lavender
Rosemary
Santolina
Wall germander

FOR INFILLING
The following will add blocks of colour:
Golden-leaved herbs
Golden marjoram
Golden feverfew
Silver-leaved herbs
Curry plant
Santolina
Variegated herbs
Variegated meadow-sweet
Variegated lemon balm
Flowering herbs
Hyssop
Sage
Wall germander

CLOSED-KNOT GARDEN
Here three types of hedging herb – box, sage and santolina – have been used to create a closed-knot pattern.

HERBS WITH PAVING

PAVING BEDDED ON SAND creates ideal conditions for herbs that like sunny, fast-draining ground. Creeping herbs such as thyme will spread out from the cracks, or you can plant self-seeders like golden feverfew to germinate in crevices. A purpose-built chequerboard pattern of slabs with herbs in the spaces between is both decorative and practical, giving easy access to each plant. Alternatively, you can plant herbs in and around existing paving (*see p.33*).

CHEQUERBOARD HERB GARDEN

This simple design makes an extremely effective showpiece for herbs, planted to create blocks of colour that highlight the design. Slabs are placed alternately with gaps over an area whose size depends on the measurements and number of the slabs used.

PLANTING TIPS
• Always include herbs with a spreading or naturally floppy habit to soften the hard edges of the paving slabs.
• A chequerboard is a good place to grow running herbs, such as mint, which will be contained by the paving slabs.

YOU NEED:

TOOLS
• Pegs, string, builder's square, straight-edge
• Spade • Rake
• Club hammer
• Hammer
• Spirit level
• Builder's trowel
• Fork

MATERIALS
• 4 planks of 10×2cm treated softwood, two of them 2.3m long and two 1.8m long
• 8 wooden pegs, 5×5×30cm
• 12 × 7cm galvanized nails
• 12 × 25kg bags of sharp (horticultural) sand
• 10 slabs, each 45×45×3cm
• 25kg ready-mixed mortar mix

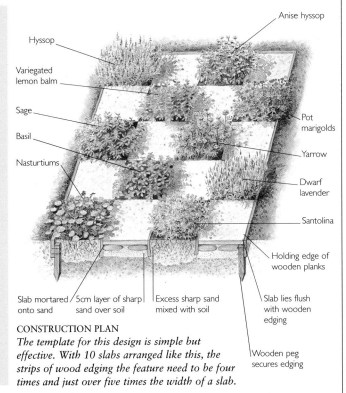

Hyssop

Variegated lemon balm

Sage

Basil

Nasturtiums

Anise hyssop

Pot marigolds

Yarrow

Dwarf lavender

Santolina

Holding edge of wooden planks

Slab lies flush with wooden edging

Wooden peg secures edging

Slab mortared onto sand

5cm layer of sharp sand over soil

Excess sharp sand mixed with soil

CONSTRUCTION PLAN
The template for this design is simple but effective. With 10 slabs arranged like this, the strips of wood edging the feature need to be four times and just over five times the width of a slab.

◄SOFT EDGES *Billowing planting and weathered slabs soon make the feature look mature.*

PREPARING THE SITE AND FRAMEWORK

1 **Mark out the perimeter** (2.3×1.85m) with string and pegs (*shown in detail on p.24*). Dig out the soil to the same depth as the edging planks (10cm); keep it for the planting spaces.

2 **Rake the area smooth** and as level as possible, removing large stones. Work backwards so that you tread on the soil as little as possible and do not compact it.

3 **Place the planks** around the edges of the rectangle, pushing them firmly in position. Hammer a peg inside one of the corners so that its top is 3cm lower than the top of the planks. Put in another peg in the same way approximately half-way along the side.

4 **Use a spirit level** to check that the tops of the planks are level. (This is very important, as the slabs must lie flush with the wooden edging.) Work your way around the rectangle, putting pegs in each of the corners and down the sides. Nail the planks to the pegs to secure them.

ADDING THE SAND AND ARRANGING THE SLABS

2 **Smooth out** and press down the sand using the straight-edge. Pull the straight-edge firmly towards you to get a level surface, and check it with a spirit level. Work backwards, to avoid treading on the sand.

1 **Cover the base** of the area with a 5cm layer of sharp sand. This helps to make a level, firm foundation for laying the paving slabs.

3 **Lay all of the** slabs in position, leaving a 45cm gap (the length of a slab) between each one. At this stage the slabs will be slightly lower than the edging to allow space for a layer of mortar. Mix the sand-cement mixture with sufficient water to make a fairly stiff mortar.

4 **Lift the slabs** one at a time and place blobs of mortar in each corner, in the middle and along the inside edge of each space. This will secure the slabs.

5 **Position each slab,** tamping it down with the handle of the club hammer against a piece of wood. Check with a spirit level, making sure the slab aligns with the frame.

PREPARING FOR PLANTING

1 **When all the slabs are laid,** scoop sand away from around their edges and seal with mortar to keep them securely in place. Allow a little time for the mortar to set.

2 **Fill the planting areas** with the retained soil, forking it over so that it is evenly mixed with the sand. Make sure the mortar is fully set before treading on the slabs to plant.

MATERIALS AND PLANTS

Paving slabs come in a wide range of colours, sizes, shapes and textures. They can be made from natural stone or cement, and can be smooth or textured. You can combine several different paving materials and shapes to create an informal effect, or you may prefer to keep the design uniform. Whatever you decide, it is always best to use materials that blend well with surrounding buildings and with the herbs you plan to plant.

SANDSTONE

YORK STONE

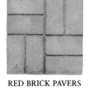

RED BRICK PAVERS

TEXTURED CEMENT

TYPES OF PAVING SLAB
Slabs are usually square or rectangular, but other shapes are available. Natural stone blends into a garden better than artificial materials, but it is expensive. Textured cement, however, gives a reasonably natural effect at much lower cost.

INFILL HERBS

Basil (*Ocimum*)
Bergamot (*Monarda*)
Borage (*Borago*)
Chamomile (*Chamaemelum*)
Chives (*Allium schoenoprasum*)
Dill (*Anethum*)
Wall germander (*Teucrium*)
Hyssop (*Hyssopus*)
Lavender (*Lavandula*)
Lemon balm (*Melissa*)
Marjoram (*Origanum*)
Mint (*Mentha*)
Nasturtiums (*Tropaeolum*)
Pot marigolds (*Calendula*)
Sage (*Salvia*)
Santolina
Tansy (*Tanacetum*)

ADAPTING EXISTING PAVING

Existing slabs can often be lifted to make planting spaces for herbs, especially if the paving is not securely laid. The soil underneath needs to be forked over and improved before planting. Or, if cracks are large enough, you can plant low-growing herbs that tolerate being occasionally trodden on.

LIFTING SLABS FROM PAVED AREAS

1 **Scrape out** and clear away any debris or old mortar around the slab. Insert a spade into the gap along one edge, then lever up the slab and remove it.

2 **Remove any hardcore** and compacted soil under the slab. Loosen and aerate the remaining soil with a fork if it is of reasonable quality, otherwise remove it.

3 **Fill the planting area** with a mixture of topsoil, compost and sharp sand. Level the surface so that it is ready for sowing seeds or planting your herbs.

PLANTING BETWEEN PAVING SLABS

HERBS IN CREVICES
Creeping thymes are ideal in paving. Plants can be inserted if gaps are wide enough, or you can sow seed (see inset). Clear out the crevice, fill with soil, water, scatter seeds and water again.

CREVICE HERBS

Compact marjoram, such as
  Origanum vulgare
  'Compactum'
Creeping mint
Creeping savory
Creeping thyme
Dwarf feverfew, such as
  Tanacetum parthenium
  'Golden Moss'
Chamomile

HERBS IN BRICK PATTERNS

BEDS EDGED WITH CLIPPED BOX look splendid, but take years to perfect. For a formal herb feature that will take only a day to build and a season to mature, use bricks to edge beds. In a wide range of textures and colours, you can use them to create all kinds of shapes and patterns, and even mix in other materials (*see pp.38–39*). Rows of bricks could be used to separate blocks of different foliage colours or types of herb, or mix plants for a less formal effect.

MAKING A HERB WHEEL

This traditional, visually effective design can be built in less than a day, and the materials used are not expensive. The lean mortar mix is used dry, so it is much easier and less messy to work with. The only preparation needed is to level and rake the site. The wheel featured here is 1.5m across, allowing plenty of room for herbs. A large plant or an ornament – perhaps a birdbath or a sundial (*see p.9*) – makes a central focal point.

YOU NEED:

TOOLS
• Rake
• Spade
• Club hammer
• Straight-edge
• Spirit level
• Trowel
• Marking pegs
• String
• Tape measure

MATERIALS
• Sand for marking out
• 50 semi-engineering bricks (22×10×6cm)
• 5 25kg bags lean mix (1 part cement to 6 parts soft sand)

PLANTING A WHEEL
Low, symmetrical planting with height in the centre would suit an island bed, but if your wheel is by a wall or in a corner, you can position taller plants towards the back.

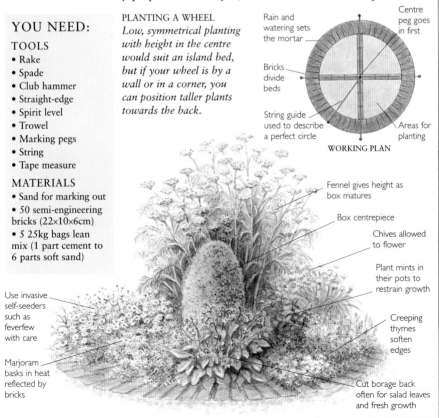

Rain and watering sets the mortar

Bricks divide beds

String guide used to describe a perfect circle

Centre peg goes in first

Areas for planting

WORKING PLAN

Fennel gives height as box matures

Box centrepiece

Chives allowed to flower

Plant mints in their pots to restrain growth

Creeping thymes soften edges

Use invasive self-seeders such as feverfew with care

Marjoram basks in heat reflected by bricks

Cut borage back often for salad leaves and fresh growth

◄ MATCHING MATERIALS *You can choose bricks to blend in with existing paths and walls.*

MARKING AND DIGGING OUT THE CIRCLE

1 **To mark out the edge** place a peg roughly in the centre of the site. Tie a length of string to the peg, and then, at half the width you want the herb bed area to be (here 70cm), tie a knot. Hold a peg against the knot and inscribe a circle around the centre peg, then trickle sand over it (*inset*) to mark it clearly.

2 **Starting on the circle** mark and working outwards, dig out a shallow trench, just wider and 5cm deeper than your bricks. This will allow plenty of space for both the bricks and the layer of dry mortar mix ("lean mix") below that secures them. Keep some of the dug-out soil for infilling later.

POSITIONING AND LAYING BRICKS

1 **Arrange all the bricks** around the trench first, so that you can adjust spacing where needed. The bigger the circle, the smaller the gaps between bricks at the outer edges will be.

2 **Spread a 5cm layer** of the lean mix over the base of the trench and, placing three or four bricks at a time, tap into position. Use a spirit level to check that they are level.

3 **To position the spokes,** divide the wheel in half by putting in 2 pegs outside it and joining them with string, which must also pass the centre peg. Repeat to make quarters and check with a builder's square.

4 **Dig trenches** for the spokes, just wider and deeper than the bricks. Set the bricks on a layer of lean mix, then pack soil up against them. You can either complete the cross, or leave a central hole for a plant.

SPACING AND PLANTING THE HERBS

Arrange the plants in their positions before you plant, then you can adjust spacing as required. Water thoroughly before removing each plant from its pot by tapping the base and pulling gently. Make planting holes and insert the plants, then water them in well. Water regularly until the young plants are fully established, especially in dry weather.

HERBS USED IN THE BEDS

3 × Bronze fennel	3 × Borage
3 × Chives	4 × Marjoram.
2 × Spearmint	5 × Chamomile
5 × Thyme	3 × Golden feverfew

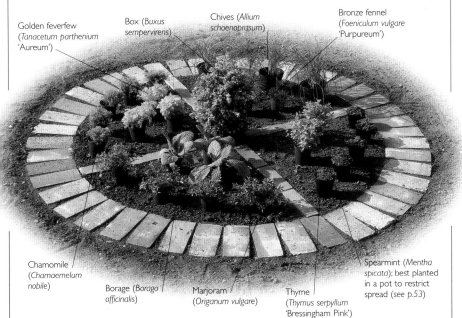

Golden feverfew
(*Tanacetum parthenium*
'Aureum')

Box (*Buxus
sempervirens*)

Chives (*Allium
schoenoprasum*)

Bronze fennel
(*Foeniculum vulgare*
'Purpureum')

Chamomile
(*Chamaemelum
nobile*)

Borage (*Borago
officinalis*)

Marjoram
(*Origanum vulgare*)

Thyme
(*Thymus serpyllum*
'Bressingham Pink')

Spearmint (*Mentha
spicata*); best planted
in a pot to restrict
spread (see p.53)

ALTERNATIVE BRICK PATTERNS

Bricks laid flat in lines, end to end, can be used to map out all sorts of designs (*see below*) at the least expense, but you can also vary the way they are laid to add interest to edging. Double rows can be laid end on, then side on for a basket-weave pattern, or diagonally herringbone-style. Try alternating bricks laid flat with bricks on their ends sticking up between them for mini-battlements, or sink them part-way into the soil at an angle for a sawtooth effect. Bricks also mix well with a variety of other materials.

STYLE DECISIONS

Always choose bricks that relate in colour and texture to the existing hard surfaces of your house and garden for a unified effect. A builder's merchant may well have a wider selection than most home-and-garden centres. The texture of the bricks is also important; smooth, new bricks could look great in a modern garden design, but rough-textured facing bricks, which already appear weathered, are more appropriate in a traditional or cottage-style setting. They also give a firmer footing; or, for a non-slip surface, use stable bricks, attractively etched with criss-crossing diagonal lines.

BUYING BRICKS

The types of brick that flake through frost damage are unsuitable for paving, but used ornamentally, they will age and "distress" quickly, if that is the look you desire.
• "Engineering" bricks, flat on both sides, are hard-wearing and frost- and damp-resistant.
• "House" bricks, usually also weatherproof, are the ones with a dent (the "frog").
• "Facing" bricks, usually shallower, are used for decorative cladding; not all can withstand severe weather. The bricks with three holes along their length are known as "cored" – with ready-made mini-planting pockets!

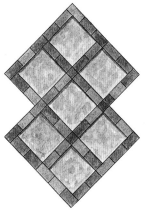

DOUBLE DIAMOND
This bold design could be set into a patio as a planting feature. You will need a builder's square to ensure true right-angles, at 90°.

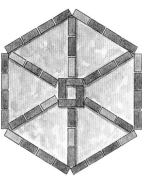

SQUARED CIRCLE
Make a circle as for a wheel and use string guides to divide it into six beds. Cut off the outer curved segments with bricks for a hexagonal shape.

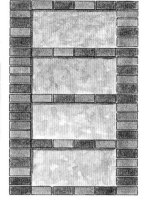

BRICK LADDER
Planted with tough creeping herbs like thymes, this ladder could be set into a not-too-frequently used path. Make sure soil and bricks are level.

COMBINING MATERIALS

Small herb-bed features provide an opportunity to introduce interesting hard landscaping materials into the garden without laying out too much money, particularly when set off by less expensive surrounds such as gravel or cobbles set in mortar. When combining more than two materials, as below, try to match at least two in colour or texture, or the result will be too busy, especially in small spaces. Modern, "antiqued" pavers and rope- or barley-twist edging are very convincing, or you might want to invest a little more in originals. Salvage yards may have small quantities of reclaimed setts or edging tiles which, because they do not interest professionals working on large projects, can be quite modestly priced.

▶ FILLING GAPS
Dyes are available to make mortars blend in, here between square setts – or you could choose a contrasting colour for a more lively effect. Make wide gaps more interesting by studding the mortar with small pebbles, seashells or even terracotta-pot or crockery shards.

LOOSE SURFACES
Use frogged bricks either face down or on their sides, especially next to soil or other materials that tend to "travel", such as gravel.

MEDITERRANEAN STYLE

THE SUN-LOVING HERBS THAT THRIVE on Mediterranean hillsides are ideally suited to hot, stony ground. A stony layer over the soil is not only a natural way to conserve moisture, but also absorbs the sun's warmth during the day to release it at night, creating a favourable "microclimate". Build a scree garden (*below*) or grow spreading herbs, like thyme, near paths or other hard surfaces, so they can inch their way into crannies or along the cracks in a flight of steps.

MAKING A SCREE GARDEN

A scree garden mimics the rocky natural landscape at the foot of a hill or cliff. It is an ideal feature for areas of low rainfall but, to make it look natural and maximize its water-saving properties, it is important to position rocks and plants as shown below. When angled correctly, the rocks channel rainwater towards the plants instead of letting it roll down the slope.

Choose rocks of a type and colour to blend into your surroundings. Good suppliers should be able to guarantee that they do not come from an area where their extraction may damage the environment – particularly important in the case of limestone. The mock tufa and reconstituted rocks now available are cheap and convincing.

PRACTICAL TIPS
• Do not use rocks too heavy for you to handle comfortably, and do not bend from the waist or use a twisting movement if lifting, as you can easily damage your back.
• For the best effect, choose a site where a wall or fence can act as backdrop.
• Select the sunniest spot possible as heat will intensify the plants' aromas.

HOW A SCREE GARDEN WORKS
It is essential that the rocks are positioned in a natural-looking way but also at an angle that gives maximum benefit to the plants.

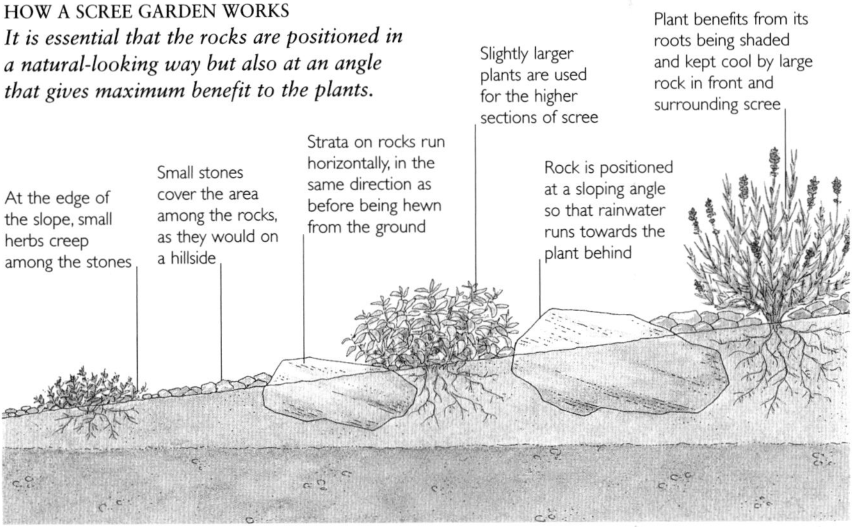

Plant benefits from its roots being shaded and kept cool by large rock in front and surrounding scree

Slightly larger plants are used for the higher sections of scree

Strata on rocks run horizontally, in the same direction as before being hewn from the ground

Rock is positioned at a sloping angle so that rainwater runs towards the plant behind

At the edge of the slope, small herbs creep among the stones

Small stones cover the area among the rocks, as they would on a hillside

◀ SCREE GARDEN *Rocks and stones provide a natural setting for sun-loving herbs.*

ARRANGING THE ROCKS

1 **Having weeded** and dug the site, spread a 2.5cm layer of sharp sand over the surface. Dig it into the soil to assist drainage.

2 **Rake soil** towards the back of the area, to create a gentle slope. Choose a gradient that is appropriate to the site.

3 **Position the large rocks,** arranging them in as naturalistic a way as possible. Some may need to be grouped together, with others set a little way apart.

4 **Dig a shallow depression** for each rock. Make sure that when in position the rock is at the correct angle to the slope (*see previous page*) and sits securely in the ground.

5 **Place the herbs,** still in their pots, in their planting positions. Make sure that the larger plants are each put behind a rock so that their roots keep cool and can absorb all the available moisture. Place small plants towards the front of the site.

Planting Herbs and Spreading Scree

1 **Dig planting holes** for the larger herbs. Ease them from their pots and plant to the correct depth. Firm the soil around each plant and water in thoroughly.

2 **Pile the larger pieces** of scree among the rocks in this part of the bed. Then, using a rake, distribute the pieces evenly over the area, taking care not to damage the plants.

4 **Cover the lower,** front part of the bed with the smallest grade of scree. Use a trowel to spread the stones carefully among and around the plants without damaging them.

3 **Use a trowel** to make planting holes for the smaller herbs. Remove from their pots, plant and water.

AROMATIC ENVIRONMENT
In the finished garden, silver-leaved herbs blend with the pale-coloured scree. The sun will draw out the herbs' full aroma. Little maintenance will be needed: remove any weeds that do appear as soon as seen.

HERBS USED

Artemisia
Lavender (several types, including French lavender, *Lavandula stoechas*)
Rosemary
Sage (including pineapple sage, *S. elegans*, and golden-variegated sage, *Salvia officinalis* 'Icterina')
Santolina
Thyme

PLANTING POSSIBILITIES

Herb plants and stones make perfect companions, not only in rock gardens and scree gardens. Paths, walls and steps all provide opportunities to use herbs that will bask in reflected warmth, while their roots creep under stones and into crevices to seek moist soil and protection from the heat of the sun. Such situations usually also offer good drainage and thus protection from winter wet, which many sun-loving herbs dislike.

PLANTING HERBS AMONG STEPS

You may have steps where a path changes in level, or you could incorporate a couple into a rock or scree garden design for interest and access. Around them, grow spreading, creeping herbs such as thymes, catmints and chamomile to soften the edges and colonize cracks (some will self-seed, too) but do trim them back from time to time so that the steps do not become dangerous, especially in wet weather.

A FIRM FOOTING
If you are planning to use rough-hewn rocks and cobbles to form steps along a path, make the treads really wide and easy to negotiate.

SAFE SURFACES
Even if steps don't go anywhere in particular, keep rocky surfaces moss- and algae-free, and don't let plants cover them completely.

BUILDING SIMPLE STEPS

Incorporating some informal steps into a sloping rock or scree garden gives you easy access to tend plants. Choose flattish stones that are of the same type and colour as the other rocks to retain the steps, cementing them in on a simple footing of rubble. Pack soil behind them and make flat treads with a layer of mortar studded with rounded pebbles, again in a matching stone. Planting pockets will really help blend the steps into the feature.

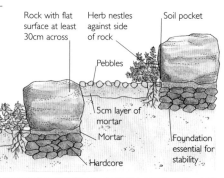

Rock with flat surface at least 30cm across

Herb nestles against side of rock

Soil pocket

Pebbles

5cm layer of mortar

Mortar

Hardcore

Foundation essential for stability

ASSOCIATING PLANTS WITH STONE

The most successful gardens not only group different plants together well, but also associate hard landscaping materials with plants to create contrasts of colour and texture. Rocks, stones, pebbles or gravel that you introduce into your garden should match what exists locally, both in terms of the soil and of building materials, and you will find, with experimentation, that certain plants not only complement but are flattered by them. A little research into the native habitat of plants can contribute to ideas for creating a landscape in which the planting looks very natural.

◄ WINDSWEPT MOOR
Tufa is a neutral, natural foil for tough, wiry, chalk-loving thymes. For a really long-established effect, you can hollow out planting pockets in this soft stone.

TUFA

► BRIGHT AND BREEZY
To accentuate a coastal feel in a planting on sandy soil, use low, sun-loving, wind-resistant plants in bold colours. Golden foliage always adds warmth and light.

SANDSTONE

◄ DARK AND HANDSOME
Slate landscapes are often associated with running water and lush growth: use vivid, vigorous foliage herbs like bronze fennel, mint and artemisia, here with sedums.

SLATE

HERBS IN CONTAINERS

WINDOWBOXES, POTS AND PLANTERS are ideal for growing herbs if space is limited. Position them wherever they are useful or look decorative – on steps, sills or secured to balcony railings. You can keep culinary herbs close to the kitchen, or use aromatic plants to scent a patio. Clipped into globes and cones (*see p.50*), box and bay make perfect centrepieces for formal gardens. Site tender and sun-loving herbs, such as basil and thymes, in the sunniest spots.

WINDOWBOX HERB GARDEN

This miniature herb bed (*left*) can be packed with plants to use all summer. They will need more care than if growing in the ground. Plant with soft-stemmed herbs that you will harvest often, such as parsley and chives, or choose small plants of larger, shrubby herbs such as rosemary, sage, marjoram and thyme and, at the end of the season, plant them out in the garden.

PLANTING A WINDOWBOX

YOU NEED:

TOOLS
• Trowel
• Bucket

MATERIALS
• Windowbox
• Drainage crocks
• Sharp sand
• Multi-purpose compost

1 **Cover the base** of the trough with a layer of broken terracotta crocks to ensure good drainage, which is essential for most herbs. (Pieces of polystyrene, a layer of chunky gravel or pebbles make good alternatives.)

2 **Using a trowel,** mix together five parts by volume potting compost to one part sharp sand.

3 **Fill the windowbox** with the compost and sand mixture until it is about two-thirds full. This should leave sufficient depth to set in small herb plants, then to pack adequate compost around their rootballs.

◀ CORE COLLECTION *A single container can provide a wide range of culinary flavours.*

POSITIONING THE PLANTS

1 **Before planting, arrange** the herbs in their pots alongside the windowbox in their approximate positions. Bear in mind heights and growth habits; for example, put trailing plants at the front. Water the plants well before removing them from their pots.

Spearmint (plant in its pot to stop it swamping other plants)

Oregano

Chives

Rosemary

PLANTS USED

1 × Chives
1 × French tarragon
1 × Garlic chives
1 × Oregano
1 × Rosemary
1 × Sage
1 × Spearmint
2 × Thyme

Garlic chives

Thyme

Sage

Thyme

French tarragon

2 **Remove each plant** from its pot only when you are ready to plant it, squeezing the sides of the pot and gently pulling it out. If you encounter any resistance, tap the pot firmly, then try again until the plant slides out easily.

3 **Make planting holes** with your hand, and insert the plants. Add more compost, to within 4–5cm of the rim (to leave room for watering). Firm around the plants, to ensure there are no air pockets, top up if necessary, then water well. As the herbs grow, water and trim or harvest regularly. At the end of the season, plant hardy herbs out in the garden.

A Herb Cascade

This unusual way of using simple clay pots can create a charming effect as the plants mature. Trailing herbs planted in the lowest tier will tumble over the sides, while silver-leaved thymes and bright marjorams can provide "ruffs" of foliage interest. Alpine strawberries, as used here, make a mouthwatering addition.

Preparing the Base

YOU NEED:

TOOLS
• Trowel

MATERIALS
• 5 terracotta pots with the following diameters: 39cm, 32cm, 27cm, 21cm and 16cm
• Broken crocks
• Compost mixture: 5 parts multi-purpose compost by volume to 1 part sharp sand

1 **Cover the base** of the largest pot with a layer of broken crocks to assist drainage. If plants are in constantly soggy compost, the roots may eventually rot.

2 **Add a generous layer** of the thoroughly mixed compost and sand, so that the crocks are completely covered. Roughly level out the surface.

Arranging the Pots

1 **Sit the next largest pot** inside, touching one side, so that the base of its rim aligns with the top of the first pot. Adjust the compost level to achieve the right height.

2 **Keeping the second pot** firm and level, fill the base pot up with the compost mixture. Firm as you fill, tapping the pot to encourage the compost to settle evenly.

3 **Repeat the process** using the other pots until the cascade is complete. Arrange the pots asymmetrically as above, to leave wider planting spaces for the herbs.

PLANTING THE TIERS

Oregano

Basil

Pot marjoram

Thyme

Alpine strawberries

Plant up each tier, starting at the bottom and spacing the herbs so that they can spread a little. Water thoroughly.

PLANTS USED

5 × Alpine strawberries
2 × Basil
2 × Pot marjoram

1 × Oregano
3 × Gold-leaved thyme
3 × Silver-leaved thyme

MORE CONTAINER IDEAS

You can use all sorts of containers for herbs, provided that they have holes for drainage in the bottom. A clipped evergreen in a good-sized pot, in balance with the size of its head of growth, will last for years, fed every spring and well watered. Closely planted herbs will need lifting and possibly renewing every year.

CLIPPED BAY TREES

You only need clip bay twice, in late spring and late summer. Bay leaves retain their flavour exceptionally well: dried and stored in an airtight container, the clippings should last all year round. A top-dressing of fresh compost and the addition of some slow-release fertilizer granules each spring will keep growth vigorous.

▶ STANDARD BAY
Bays can be bought as standards to make long-lasting feature plants. Variegated thymes make a fine underplanting.

OTHER HERBS FOR SHAPING

Bay makes the most effective standard plants, but other shrubby herbs can be grown clipped into neat bun-shapes for formal display. Choose any of the plants recommended for formal edging (*see p.27*).

Using a Strawberry Pot

These attractive planters are equally suited to growing herbs, and also use space to best advantage. Choose small-size pots of herbs, so that, holding the top-growth gently bunched in one hand, you can insert the rootballs through the planting holes in the side. Do not fill the pot completely with compost, then try to force the plants in through the side: add a layer of compost up to the level of the first hole, then plant, then add another layer, and so on (*see below left*). Then plant the top layer.

◀ PLANT CARE
Keep terracotta pots well watered from the top, as the compost around the planting holes can easily dry out through the porous terracotta.

▼ PLANTING UP IN STAGES
With one hand in and one hand out of the planter, ease in the plants and firm compost up, under and around their rootballs.

Fill pot to the base of the lip

Herb's root ball well within hole

Tuck compost in under plant

One part sand to six parts multi-purpose compost

Drainage crocks

GOOD MIXERS
Alpine strawberries, which are not too vigorous, make perfect partners in this pot for tarragon, rosemary, savory and marjoram.

A Herb Tower

This tall wire basket has been converted into a planter by lining it with a thick layer of sphagnum moss (felt or fibre hanging-basket liner makes a good substitute), then polythene pierced with plenty of holes at the base. Add a layer of crocks at the base, then fill with a free-draining compost, as for other containers. You can use wire-cutters to snip out planting holes in the side (not too many, or you will weaken the structure), being sure to clip off or bend over any spikes of wire for safety. Plant creeping herbs such as thyme around the sides to trail down and give the tower a truly organic look. Keep it well watered.

Chives

Purple sage

Marjoram

Thyme

Pineapple mint

LOOKING AFTER HERB PLANTS

PREPARING AND PLANTING

Herbs do not demand lots of nourishment; provided the ground has been dug over and weeded they will grow happily without additional fertilizers. Choose plants to match your soil (*below*), and water them well on planting and during their first spring and summer, particularly in hot spells. Given a good start, these easy-going plants should prove easy to tend and trouble-free.

WHICH HERBS FOR YOUR SOIL?

To save yourself the most work, choose herbs that will enjoy your garden soil. Feverfew, parsley, chives and mint like rich, cool soil, but in heavy ground in a cold, wet winter, the roots of sun-loving herbs such as rosemary, sage and lavender may rot away. You can improve a heavy soil on planting (*below*), but light soil will need continual bulking up with organic matter.

GROWING TIP

If your soil is unsuitable for certain herbs, consider growing them in containers. Tough, sun-loving herbs will be happy in a light, gritty compost and will tolerate a certain amount of summer neglect. Leafy herbs like parsley need dark, spongy, moisture-retentive compost and plenty of watering.

IMPROVING DRAINAGE

Mediterranean herbs like to snake their roots through free-draining, stony ground. To lighten up a clay soil, add plenty of sand or grit, preferably over the whole planting area before you plant it up, or by working it into the base and sides of planting holes. You must use sharp sand (not soft builder's sand, which clumps together and spoils the soil's texture); this may be called "garden" or "horticultural" sand at DIY or garden centres. Similarly, choose "garden" grit (which may be found in the alpine plant or rock garden section of a garden centre). This has been washed free of lime, which many of these plants dislike.

SHARP SAND

COARSE GRIT

ADDING SAND OR GRIT
Mix in the drainage material well before you plant. The heavier the soil, the more sand or grit will be required.

Spacing and Planting Out Young Plants

Close planting means that beds will fill out quickly, but tends to lead to more work as plants begin to crowd each other. Wide spacing will leave gaps in which weeds are likely to grow. Check plant labels to see what the eventual spread and height of each plant will be, and space appropriately.

TIPS FOR SMALL SPACES

• To relieve crowding, you need to lift plants and divide or even replace them. Pruning will only make them grow even more vigorously.
• Check labels to look for smaller or more slow-growing varieties of the herbs you want.

ARRANGING AND PLANTING
Arrange the herbs in their pots first, giving each enough room to grow and considering how much you want them to spill over the edges of the planting area. Water the herbs, plant and firm in, then water again.

Controlling Invasive Herbs

Some herbs, especially mints, can spread at a rapid rate, swamping other plants. The best way to restrict them is to plant them in a sunken pot, providing a physical barrier so that spreading roots cannot escape. Divide the plants each spring and refill the pot with fresh soil or compost or a combination of the two, then replant.

1 **Dig a hole** large enough to hold a big container with drainage holes. Place it in the hole and add compost.

2 **Plant the herb** (*here mint*) in the pot and firm. Add enough compost to cover the pot's rim and water well.

INVASIVE HERBS

Herbs that, in small spaces, need to be kept in check and regularly divided (*see p.57*) include:
Comfrey
Marjoram
Mint
Tarragon (especially Russian)
Tansy
Thyme
Sweet woodruff

CARING FOR HERBS

Healthy young plants are quick to thrive and, if they have been planted carefully in well-prepared soil, will require little aftercare. Water well for the first few weeks; if the soil is merely dampened, roots stay near the surface instead of penetrating deep into the ground. Once established, harvest leaves and shoots regularly to encourage bushy, fresh growth.

ENCOURAGING HEALTHY PLANTS

Few popular herbs are big feeders, but if harvested heavily and often they may need an all-purpose feed. Pinching out shoot tips will encourage leafy herbs to produce plenty of fresh foliage, while shrubby herbs need trimming once or twice a year to keep them in good shape. With some herbs it is better to remove flowers in bud to preserve a good flavour; others need deadheading.

TIPS FOR GOOD GROWTH

• Do not harvest newly planted herbs until they are established and making new growth.
• Grow sufficient quantities of culinary favourites (*see pp.12–15*) so that plants do not suffer from being cut too hard, too often.
• During hot or windy weather, make sure that herbs in pots receive sufficient water.

TRIMMING
*Trim grey-leaved herbs like lavender twice a year. In autumn, remove dead flowers and cut back leggy stems (*right*). The following spring, clip stems by at least 2.5cm of the previous year's growth (*far right), making sure some foliage remains.*

KEEPING HERBS IN GOOD SHAPE

NIPPING BUDS	DEADHEADING	PINCHING OUT	PRUNING
Remove flower buds to prevent bitterness in cooking: **Basil, lovage, parsley, rocket, salad burnet, tarragon.** Remove flower buds from **chives** to encourage new foliage (although if you let them flower you can use the flowerheads in salads and omelettes).	Deadhead to prevent self-seeding: **Angelica, borage, dill, evening primroses, fennel, feverfew, garlic chives, lemon balm.** Deadhead to prolong flowering season: **Borage, catmint, nasturtiums, pot marigolds.**	Pinch out or harvest regularly to promote bushy new foliage: **Basil, lemon balm, lovage, marjoram, mint, parsley, sage, salad burnet, sweet cicely, thyme.** Leggy lemon balms, chives and mints can be cut back with shears to encourage fresh new growth.	Trim twice a year (*see above*) to keep plants in good shape: **Curry plant, lavender, winter savory, santolina.** Cut back almost to ground level once or twice in the growing season to prolong the life of the plants: **Angelica, fennel, marjoram, mint.**

Growing Herbs for Winter Use

While most herbs are harvested from spring to autumn, dying down over winter outside, some can be lifted (*below*) and grown inside on a windowsill or in a greenhouse. Pots of late summer-sown herbs (*see overleaf*) such as coriander and parsley will grow well on a warm, sunny sill. Evergreen herbs such as bay can be harvested from the garden throughout winter. Although there will be no fresh growth, weather-beaten sprigs are still flavoursome.

SUPERMARKET POTS

The small pots of growing herbs now readily available from supermarkets can be used to supplement winter supplies and also provide a source of new plants. The pots usually contain a cluster of small plantlets, which are too crowded to survive long. Carefully ease these out of the pot and split them into small plugs, keeping plenty of compost attached to their roots. Pot up, water thoroughly, and grow on a light windowsill.

1 Herbs that die down in winter can be lifted for winter use. Choose a dry day in early autumn and, using a fork, lift a mature clump of herbs (*here chives*) from the garden.

2 Divide the clump into smaller pieces with your hands. If the plant is tough, use a small, sharp garden knife. Shake firmly to remove loose soil from around the roots.

3 Plant up the divided pieces into pots or deep trays of potting compost. Stand them in a saucer or dish of water and allow them to drink their fill.

4 Cut back any top-growth. Once the leaves have grown to about 10cm, start to harvest them regularly in order to encourage plenty of fresh growth.

HERBS IN WINTER

Evergreens that can be harvested outside all through winter:
Bay, rosemary, sage thyme, winter savory.

Herbs that can be lifted and brought inside:
Chives, scented pelargoniums, marjoram, mint, parsley, tarragon.

Herbs to sow and grow on a windowsill:
Basil, chervil, coriander, lemon balm, nasturtiums, parsley, rocket.

GROWING YOUR OWN PLANTS

THE MAJORITY OF HERBS can be grown from seed – this method is inexpensive and produces lots of plants. Taking cuttings ensures new plants that are identical to their parents. Division is both easy and a useful way of checking the spread of some herbs. To ensure that newly raised plants are large enough to survive planting out, wait for the root tips to show at the base of the pot.

SOWING SEED

Seed can be sown in containers to produce herbs that are then planted out, or directly into the open ground; check the back of packets for advice. It can also be sown in

1 **Lightly firm** some multi-purpose compost and scatter over the seeds. Cover with a light sprinkling of sieved compost. Use a watering can with a fine rose to water in well.

cracks between paving stones (*see p.33*). Spring is the best time for sowing seed, although hardy annuals such as borage may be sown outside in the autumn.

2 **Keep the tray** out of direct sunlight, on a windowsill or in a cold frame, watering or misting regularly. If spring is still cool, slip the tray into a pierced plastic bag to keep the compost warm. When the seedlings start to appear, thin them to about 5cm apart.

3 **When their first leaves** are fully unfurled, carefully lift the seedlings and replant them into small pots of fresh compost, carefully holding them by their leaves. Put them back in the frame or on the sill and grow on until large enough to plant out.

TAKING STEM-TIP CUTTINGS

Many shrubby herbs are easily grown from cuttings taken in late spring or early summer. After 6–8 weeks, tap out the pot weekly to see if roots are growing; if so, move each into its own pot and grow on until large enough to plant out.

1 **Select** non-flowering shoots (*here lemon balm*) and cut cleanly just below a leaf joint, 6 leaves down. Trim off the lower leaves.

2 **Make holes** with a dibber, insert the cuttings into firmed cuttings compost (half peat or peat substitute, half sharp sand). Firm in and water.

3 **Make a tent** with canes and a pierced plastic bag to keep an even temperature and conserve moisture. Place in a frame or on a shaded sill.

DIVIDING AND MULTIPLYING

For many herbs, dividing is a useful way of creating new plants from older ones that have lost their vigour and become woody and unproductive. Herbs are best divided in early spring or autumn, when not in full growth. Frosty days should be avoided as it is difficult to re-establish the divided pieces successfully in very cold soil.

1 **Insert a fork** well under the plant and lift it clear from the ground. Take care not to damage the roots.

2 **Trim back** heavy top-growth on the sections that you wish to keep, but always leave some foliage.

3 **Divide the clump** into pieces, keeping only the younger, healthier sections complete with their roots.

4 **Plant the pieces,** spacing them to allow for future spread. Water in and keep the soil moist until established.

ENCOURAGING NEW PLANTLETS

The stems of shrubby herbs, such as thyme and sage, can be encouraged to develop roots by heaping soil mixed with sharp sand and potting compost around the base of the plant in spring, leaving only the shoot tips showing. In late summer or autumn, rooted stems around the plant's edge can be cut off and potted up or planted.

PROPAGATION METHODS FOR POPULAR HERBS

GROWING FROM SEED		CUTTINGS	DIVISION
Angelica	Marjoram	Bay	Bergamot
Basil	Nasturtium	French tarragon	Chives
Borage	Parsley	Hyssop	Fennel
Chervil	Pot marigold	Lavender	French tarragon
Chives	Rocket	Lemon verbena	Lemon balm
Coriander	Sage	Marjoram	Lovage
Dill	Sorrel	Mint	Marjoram
Fennel	Savory	Rosemary	Mint
Hyssop	Sweet cicely	Sage	Thyme
Lemon balm	Thyme	Thyme	
Lovage		Winter savory	

DRYING AND STORING HERBS

MANY HERBS CAN BE DRIED to make anything from a pot-pourri to a *bouquet garni* that will add piquancy to a winter casserole. Herbs can also be preserved fresh, to bring back a reminder of the scents and flavours of summer. Choose only healthy sprigs while plants are in growth; in autumn, harvest herbaceous herbs to store before they die back or are cut down by frost.

HERBS FOR DRYING

Herbs from hot climates, such as sage, rosemary and thyme, dry especially well. Soft-leaved herbs, such as basil, take far longer to dry and some of the flavour may be lost.

Herbs can be air-dried (*below*) in a warm, well-ventilated room. Hang them up or lay out on a rack. They can also be dried in a microwave on a high setting for about four minutes. Alternatively, dry gently in an oven at the very lowest setting. For flavour, fennel, lovage, mint, rosemary, sage, tarragon and thyme are best picked before flowering. Hyssop and marjoram should be picked while in flower, while others such as fennel and caraway can be left to produce their spicy, flavoursome seeds.

HARVEST FROM THE GARDEN
Pick herbs for storing early in the day, after any dew or rain has dried. Avoid crushing the leaves in order to preserve their volatile oils.

1 **Most herbs** (*here lemon balm*) are most easily dried on the stem. Tie into small bunches and hang them upside down in a well-ventilated room or airing cupboard.

2 **When the leaves** are brittle and break easily, rub them off the stems onto a sheet of dry paper. Crumble pieces together if you are using the entire plant.

3 **Transfer the dried herbs** to an airtight container, such as a screw-top jar. Use a jar made of coloured glass – this helps prevent oxidization, which mars the flavour.

POPULAR HERBS FOR DRYING

Angelica Stems, leaves and seeds
Bay Leaves
Bergamot Leaves and flowers
Borage Leaves
Catnip, catmint Leaves and flowers
Chamomile Flowers
Chervil Leaves
Chives Leaves and flowers
Coriander Seeds
Curry plant Leaves and flowers
Dill Leaves and seeds
Fennel Leaves and seeds
Geraniums, scented Leaves

Lavender Flowers
Lemon balm Leaves
Lemon verbena Leaves
Lovage Leaves and seeds
Marjoram Leaves and flowers
Mint Leaves
Pot marigold Flowers
Rosemary Leaves
Sage Leaves and flowers
Savory Leaves
Tarragon Leaves
Thyme Leaves and flowers
Yarrow Leaves and flowers

OTHER WAYS OF PRESERVING HERBS

Soft-leaved herbs such as basil, chives, chervil, fennel and dill retain a better flavour if frozen. Seal them in small plastic bags or, alternatively, lay them in an ice-cube tray, chopping them first if necessary. Top up with water and freeze. Highly aromatic herbs can be preserved in oil, vinegar, syrup or brandy, imparting their flavour to the liquid at the same time. Herb vinegars are versatile and will keep for several years, becoming more mellow as they age. Use a good wine or cider vinegar.

FREEZING SPRIGS
Freezing is a good way to preserve herbs, and is especially suited to those with fine or soft leaves. Place whole sprigs in a plastic bag, seal and freeze.

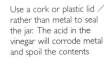

HERBS IN VINEGAR
This vinegar combines the flavours of dill and anise, delicious used in a salad dressing or in a fish dish. Lightly crush the herbs before putting in the bottle. Add the vinegar and leave to steep for at least three weeks.

Borage flowers

Use a cork or plastic lid rather than metal to seal the jar. The acid in the vinegar will corrode metal and spoil the contents

Dill

HERB ICE CUBES
Some herbs, such as borage and mint, can be used to flavour drinks. Chop the herbs (leaving decorative flowers whole), place in an ice-cube tray, fill with water and freeze.

Anise

A CATALOGUE OF HERBS

THIS CATALOGUE PROVIDES A GUIDE to some of the most popular herbs. Descriptions include suggestions for how plants might be used in the garden, as well as in cooking, with tips on preserving and propagating them. Symbols indicate each herb's preferred growing conditions and hardiness.

☼ *Prefers full sun* ☼ *Prefers partial shade* ▦ *Tolerates full shade* ◊ *Prefers well-drained soil*
◊ *Prefers moist soil* ◦ *Prefers wet soil* ✿ *Half-hardy* ✿✿ *Frost hardy* ✿✿✿ *Fully hardy*
♀ *RHS Award of Garden Merit* **Large** *Taller than 1.2m* **Medium** *60cm–1.2m* **Small** *Up to 60cm*

A

Achillea millefolium
Yarrow
A small, mat-forming perennial, bearing flattened flowerheads in white, cream or pale pink in summer. The fern-like grey-green leaves are aromatic when crushed. Deeper pink or red yarrows

PINK-FLOWERED YARROW
'LILAC BEAUTY'

make attractive border plants. Flowers last well when cut.
Uses Medicinally, it is used to staunch cuts and reduce fever. Contact may irritate some skins. Flowers can be dried for decoration.
Cultivation Can be invasive. Divide in autumn or spring, sow seed in spring.
☼ ◊ ✿✿✿

Agastache foeniculum
Anise hyssop
Spikes of blue-purple flowers open from mid-summer to early autumn. A medium-sized perennial, it makes an attractive border plant.
Uses The aniseed-flavoured leaves can be used in salads or as a sweetener. Medicinally, the plant is used to treat coughs. Preserve by drying.
Cultivation Needs a sheltered site to survive winters in cold areas. Sow seed in spring, divide in spring, or take cuttings in early summer.
☼ ◊ ✿✿

Agrimonia eupatoria
Agrimony
A medium-sized perennial with slender spikes of small, sweet-smelling yellow flowers in summer. Best suited to an informal border or wildflower meadow. Attracts bees.
Uses Dried flowers add a honey scent to pot-pourri. Medicinally, it is prescribed for mild digestive problems, sore throats and catarrh and some skin conditions.
Cultivation Sow seed in spring, divide in spring or autumn.
☼ ◊ ✿✿✿

AGRIMONY

◀ORNAMENTAL VALUES *Globe-shaped alliums and box harmonize with purple sage and lavender.*

ALLIUM: Chives, garlic, onions

Some alliums are grown for their flowers, others to flavour food. A few are perfect in both roles.

A. schoenoprasum
Chives
Small perennial, with round heads of usually pink-purple flowers in early summer. The leaves are tubular and taste mildly of onions.
Uses Use leaves in salads, sauces and to flavour many cooked dishes. Preserve by freezing or drying.
Cultivation Sow seed in spring, divide in autumn or spring. Easily grown in containers. Lift and pot for indoor winter use (*see p.55*).
▣ ◊◊ ✽✽✽

A. tuberosum
Garlic/Chinese chives
In late summer, clusters of white flowers are carried above the clumps of strap-shaped, garlic-flavoured leaves. A small perennial.

CHIVES

RAMSONS

Uses As chives, and in stir-fries and Chinese cooking.
Cultivation As chives.
▣ ◊◊ ✽✽✽

A. sativum
Garlic
A medium-sized bulbous perennial, if unharvested, with clusters of bell-shaped flowers in summer.
Uses Bulbs are used in cooking worldwide. Medicinally, it helps fight infections, especially colds.
Cultivation Harvest in late summer and early autumn; store bulbs in a cool place. Plant individual cloves for new plants in autumn or winter.
▣ ◊ ✽✽✽

Other alliums
Onion, *A. cepa*: an essential ingredient for cooking, but also used in dyeing.
Ramsons or wild garlic, *A. ursinum*: perennial for lightly shaded wild gardens; it is often found growing in woodland areas. White flowers open in late spring.

Aloysia triphylla ♥
Lemon verbena
The leaves of this deciduous, medium-sized to large shrub have a strong lemon aroma. Spikes of tiny white flowers appear in summer.
Uses Fresh leaves can be used to flavour drinks, and both sweet and savoury dishes. Leaves can also be dried for infusions or pot-pourris. It is used in aromatherapy.
Cultivation Protect in a cold greenhouse or conservatory in cold areas in winter. Suitable for growing in containers.
▣ ◊ ✽✽

Alpine (wild) strawberry
see Fragaria

Anethum graveolens
Dill
A medium-sized annual with feathery foliage and flattened heads of yellow flowers.
Uses Leaves and seeds are delicious in potato, egg and seafood dishes. Medicinally, it aids digestion. Freeze or dry leaves to preserve; dry seeds.
Cultivation Sow seed from spring to summer for a continuous supply. Runs to seed quickly in dry soil.
▣ ◊ ✽✽✽

DILL

ANGELICA

CHERVIL

Angelica archangelica
Angelica

Large, statuesque plant with domed heads of tiny yellow-green flowers in summer. Usually grown as a biennial.
Uses The aromatic leaves can be eaten in salads or infused as a tea; the roots and seeds are added to liqueurs. Crystallized stems are used to decorate confectionery. Medicinal uses include easing bronchial congestion and digestive problems. Stems, leaves and seeds can be preserved by drying.
Cultivation Sow seed *in situ* as soon as it ripens or in spring. Cutting flowerheads to prevent seeds forming may prolong the life of the plant and prevents self-seeding.
◼ ◊ ✴✴✴

Anise hyssop *see*
Agastache

Anthriscus cerefolium
Chervil

A small, pretty annual with fern-like leaves and tiny white flowers in mid-summer. It grows well in a cool site but tends to run to seed in full sun.

Uses The aniseed-flavoured leaves are a traditional ingredient of *fines herbes* in French cooking; they can also be added to potato, egg or fish dishes. Medicinally, chervil is prescribed to soothe inflamed eyes. Preserve leaves by freezing or drying.
Cultivation For a continuous supply of leaves, sow seed in succession from spring to autumn. Can be grown in a container in light shade.
◼ ◊ ✴✴✴

Apium graveolens
Wild celery, smallage

An ancestor of the cultivated celery that is grown for the table. Loose heads of tiny, greenish-white flowers are carried on medium-sized plants with divided leaves. Can be annual or biennial. Suitable for informal herb gardens.
Uses Seldom used in cooking, although the seeds are sometimes used to flavour salt. Medicinally, it is prescribed to ease indigestion.
Cultivation Sow seed in spring.
◼◼ ◊ ✴✴

Artemisia
Artemisia

Most artemisias have aromatic, divided, silver or grey-green leaves and many are grown purely for their ornamental effect. Most thrive in sunny sites with poor soil.
A. dracunculus
French tarragon

A large, upright perennial with narrow green leaves that have a mint-anise flavour. The type called Russian tarragon (*A. dracunculus dracunculoides*) is hardier but it has a coarser taste and can be invasive.
Uses Especially good with chicken and egg dishes. Pick leaves before flowering. Preserve by drying or freezing.
Cultivation Protect in severe winters in cold areas. Take cuttings or divide plants in late spring or early summer.
◼ ◊ ✴✴
Other artemisias

A. abrotanum, southernwood: upright shrub, usually deciduous, with finely cut, aromatic grey-green leaves. Cut back in early spring to keep in shape.

A. absinthum, absinthe: medium-sized, woody-based perennial, once the bitter element in the liqueur absinthe. Suitable for mixed borders.

A. ludoviciana, Western mugwort: medium-sized, spreading perennial with attractive silvery leaves.

RUSSIAN
TARRAGON

BORAGE

B

Basil *see Ocimum*

Bay *see Laurus*

Bergamot *see Monarda*

Borago officinalis
Borage
Medium-to-large annual, ideal for informal plantings. Blue star-shaped flowers appear in summer. The coarse leaves taste of cucumber.
Uses Fresh leaves and flowers are added to salads and drinks, such as fruit punches. Flowers can also be candied. Medicinally, borage acts as a mild sedative. Preserve leaves by drying or freezing; flowers can be frozen in ice cubes.
Cultivation Sow seed in spring or autumn. Cut old flowerheads to prevent self-seeding.
🗌 ◊ ❋❋❋

Buxus
Box
Much used as an edging in formal herb gardens, this slow-growing, evergreen shrub is ideally suited to clipping and is also excellent for topiary. The classic choice for growing as low hedges is small-leaved *B. sempervirens* 'Suffruticosa' ♥; 'Argenteo-variegata' and 'Aureovariegata' are also good for edging, with silver- and gold-edged leaves respectively.
Uses Leaves are toxic if eaten and used only in homeopathy.
Cultivation Clip to shape regularly; will eventually grow into a large shrub (or small tree) if left untrimmed.
🗌 ◊ ❋❋❋

C–D

Calendula officinalis
Pot marigold
A small, brightly coloured annual with yellow or orange flowers throughout summer and autumn. Marigolds also come in cream and tawny shades. Perfect for cottage garden-style plantings.
Uses Fresh or dried flowers can be used to give food a tangy flavour and golden colour. The leaves can also be added to salads. The flowers can be boiled to make a dye.

POT MARIGOLD

Medicinally, the plant is soothing and antiseptic, and is included in many proprietary lotions. Preserve the flowers by drying.
Cultivation Sow seed *in situ* in autumn or spring. Dead-head to prolong flowering and restrict self-seeding.
🗌 ◊ ❋❋❋

Carum carvi
Caraway
A small-to-medium upright biennial with feathery, aromatic, bright green foliage. The open heads of tiny white flowers are followed by ribbed brown seeds if the summer is sufficiently long and warm.
Uses Young leaves give salads and soups a mild, dill-like flavour. The pungent seeds are much used in eastern European cooking, especially in bread and confectionery. Medicinally, caraway is prescribed to ease digestion.
Cultivation Sow seed *in situ* from late spring to late summer. May self-seed. It can be grown in pots indoors.
🗌 ◊ ❋❋❋

Catmint, catnip *see Nepeta*

CARAWAY

Chamaemelum nobile
Chamomile
The feathery leaves of this small perennial are strongly scented when crushed. White daisy flowers appear in summer. The double-flowered 'Flore Pleno' makes a pretty edging. Low-growing forms are used to make small lawns (not hard-wearing) or seats.
Uses The flowers make a tea that acts as a mild sedative. Medicinally, it is prescribed for bronchial congestion. Preserve flowers by drying.
Cultivation Divide plants in spring or sow seed *in situ*. Choose the non-flowering 'Treneague' for lawns, spacing plants 10cm apart.
◼ ◊ ✱✱✱

Chervil *see Anthriscus*

Chives *see Allium*

Comfrey *see Symphytum*

Coriandrum sativum
Coriander
An upright, small-to-medium annual. Lower leaves resemble parsley but become thread-like higher up the plant. Clusters of tiny white flowers

CORIANDER

are borne from mid-summer to autumn, followed by seedheads full of round, pale brown seeds.
Uses The fresh, tangy leaves are a widely used flavouring, especially in Middle Eastern and Southeast Asian cooking. The seeds are used in numerous dishes including curries and pickles, as well as in spirits such as gin and Chartreuse. Medicinally, seeds are taken for minor digestive problems. Their oil can help to relieve painful joints. Preserve leaves by freezing; seeds by drying.
Cultivation Sow *in situ* from spring to early summer. Grow in full sun to produce seeds and in part shade for foliage, otherwise plants run to seed without forming many leaves.
◼◼ ◊ ✱✱✱

Cotton lavender *see Santolina*

Crocus sativus
Saffron
A small crocus that needs long, hot summers to flower.
Uses The long orange stigmas in the centre of the flower are dried to make saffron, which flavours and adds a rich gold

SAFFRON CROCUS

ROCKET

colour to Mediterranean dishes such as paella and risotto.
Cultivation Sow seed as soon as it ripens or separate offsets from corms in late spring.
◼ ◊ ✱✱✱

Curry plant *see Helichrysum*

Dill *see Anethum*

E

Eruca vesicaria subsp. *sativa*
Rocket
A popular salad plant, the leaves of this fast-growing, small-to-medium annual can be ready to pick a month after sowing.
Uses Leaves add a peppery tang to salads and sauces. Pick young before their flavour coarsens.
Cultivation Sow batches *in situ* from late winter to early summer, and again in late summer. Will self-seed. Can be grown in containers.
◼ ◊ ✱✱

Evening primrose *see Oenothera*

F–G

Fennel *see Foeniculum*

Feverfew *see Tanacetum*

Filipendula ulmaria
Meadowsweet

An elegant, medium-sized perennial for damp gardens, often found growing wild in waterside meadows. The heads of tiny cream flowers have a sweet, marzipan-like scent; the lobed, dark green leaves have a sharper aroma. 'Variegata' has leaves splashed with yellow, fading to cream as the flowers form.
Uses Medicinally, it is prescribed for pain relief and gastric upsets. Once grown as a strewing herb. The dried flowers and leaves are used in pot-pourris.
Cultivation Divide plants in autumn or spring.
▣ ◊ ✳✳✳

MEADOWSWEET

FENNEL

Foeniculum vulgare
Fennel

A large plant with stems of feathery foliage that add grace and height to any style of garden. Flat heads of tiny yellow flowers are borne in summer. Bronze-coloured 'Purpureum' is particularly decorative. Plants can be biennial or perennial.
Uses The aniseed-flavoured leaves and seeds are widely used in cooking, the leaves especially with oily fish. Medicinally, fennel is taken as a breath freshener and to ease digestion. Preserve the leaves by freezing or drying; the seeds by drying.
Cultivation Sow seed in spring. Plants self-seed freely.
▣ ◊ ✳✳✳

Fragaria vesca
Alpine or wild strawberry

A low-growing perennial with small, sweet fruit in summer following the white flowers. Can be grown in pots or in mixed beds or borders. Makes a dainty edging for paths.
Uses The fruit, delicious fresh, can be preserved in jams and syrups. Medicinally, it is mildly diuretic. Leaves and roots are used dried to relieve digestive problems. Harvest leaves in early summer.
Cultivation Sow seed in spring. Enrich soil beforehand with organic matter such as garden compost. Plants tend to deteriorate and need renewing after a few years.
▣▣ ◊ ✳✳✳

French tarragon *see Artemisia dracunculus*

Galium odoratum
Sweet woodruff

A small, spreading perennial with starry white flowers in spring and early summer. Good ground cover in shade.
Uses Dried leaves, smelling of new-mown hay, are added to pot-pourris and pillows. Fresh leaves are also used in *Maitrank* (May bowl), a German wine punch.

SWEET WOODRUFF

SUNFLOWER

Medicinally, it acts as a mild diuretic and laxative.
Cultivation Divide in spring to make more plants.
☒ ◊ ✳✳✳

Garlic, garlic chives
see Allium

H

Helianthus annuus
Sunflower
With its huge golden flowers in summer, this large, fast-growing annual makes a bold plant for a herb garden.
Uses The seeds are delicious raw or roasted and are widely used in baking. They can also be sprouted and added to salads. Medicinally, they are prescribed to relieve coughs and gastric problems. Harvest in autumn.
Cultivation To grow the tallest plants, enrich soil with well-rotted manure or garden compost prior to sowing. Sow seed *in situ*; delay sowing until late spring to avoid seedlings being killed by frost.
☒ ◊ ✳✳

Helichrysum italicum ♀
Curry plant ·
A small to medium-sized shrubby evergreen whose silvery, needle-like leaves have a sweetish curry scent. Small, flattened yellow flowerheads appear from summer to autumn. *H. italicum* 'Nanum' is a dwarf version.
Uses The flowers dry well, and can be used in winter arrangements. Dried flowers and leaves can be added to pot-pourris. The leaves add a mild curry flavour to rice, vegetables and savoury dishes.
Cultivation Cut back in spring to keep plants in good shape, taking out any winter-damaged shoots. Plants are more likely to survive winters in cold areas if drainage is good. Sow seed in autumn or spring.
☒ ◊ ✳✳

Hypericum perforatum
St John's wort
In summer, this medium-sized perennial bears star-shaped yellow flowers. Its mid-green leaves have large translucent dots that contain the oil used in herbal remedies.
Uses Externally, it is used to sooth burns, bruises, sprains and cramp. St John's wort is also prescribed to treat anxiety and nervous tension.
NB Foliage is harmful if eaten.
Cultivation Sow seed in spring, or make new plants by detaching rooted runners in spring or autumn.
☒ ◊ ✳✳✳

DWARF CURRY PLANT (*H. ITALICUM* 'NANUM')

ST JOHN'S WORT

WHITE-FLOWERED HYSSOP (*H. OFFICINALIS* F. *ALBUS*)

Hyssopus officinalis
Hyssop

A delightful small, semi-evergreen shrub, perfect for cottage gardens. The spikes of tubular flowers, in varying shades of blue, or sometimes pink or white, appear from mid-summer to autumn and are attractive to bees. *H. officinalis* subsp. *aristatus* is a dwarf hyssop suitable for rock gardens or containers, or as a low edging for beds and borders.

Uses The flowerheads and young leaves dry well and can be added to pot-pourris. The leaves have a rather bitter, sage-like flavour and can be used sparingly with meat, especially game, and in bean and lentil dishes. Hyssop is also a flavouring in liqueurs such as Chartreuse. The oil is soothing when added to a bath. Medicinally, hyssop has a range of uses, but the oil is toxic if taken in quantity, and its use is restricted by law in some countries.

Cultivation Cut back in spring to keep plants shapely. Sow seed in autumn or spring.
▣ ◊ ✻✻✻

I

Isatis tinctoria
Woad

This large, tap-rooted biennial or short-lived perennial has long been cultivated for its blue dye, although it may not be the plant reputedly used by ancient Britons to colour their skin. It can make an attractive garden plant, with its grey-green leaves and clusters of yellow flowers in summer, followed by black seeds.

Uses Medicinally, used to reduce inflammation and fever, and reputedly has anti-cancer effects. Dye plant.

Cultivation Sow seed in autumn or spring. Self-sown seedlings are best transplanted to a fresh site.
▣ ◊ ✻✻✻

L

Laurus nobilis ♀
Bay

Native to the Mediterranean, this evergeen large shrub or tree makes a handsome architectural plant for a herb garden, especially if trained as a mop-headed standard. It withstands regular clipping and is suitable for growing in containers. The leaves are a glossy green, and clusters of greenish-yellow flowers appear in spring. There is also a bay with golden leaves.

Uses The leaves are much used in cooking, usually dried, and are an essential ingredient of a *bouquet garni*. They can be added to sauces, stews, soups and even desserts. Dry leaves whole; they keep their flavour for up to a year. Medicinally, bay eases aches caused by sprains, bruises and rheumatism.

Cultivation Once established, plants are reasonably hardy, but shelter them from cold winter winds which can brown the leaves. In cold areas, plants growing in containers are best moved into a greenhouse or conservatory in winter.
▣ ◊ ✻✻

Lemon balm *see Melissa*

Lemon verbena *see Aloysia*

BAY

LAVANDULA: Lavender

Invaluable for the fragrance of their late summer flowers and silver, grey or green foliage, these small to medium-sized shrubs can be grown in mixed borders, as low hedges and in pots.

L. angustifolia
Common lavender
Compact, with flowers in mauve, pink or white. Purple 'Hidcote' ♥ is good for hedging and edging.
Uses Dried flowers are used in pot-pourris, to scent linen, and for winter decoration.

The essential oil is used in aromatherapy, perfume and cosmetics and, medicinally, as an insect repellent and to soothe burns and stings.
Cultivation Trim in early spring to keep in shape but do not cut into old wood.
🔲 ◊ ✳✳✳

Other lavenders
English lavender,
L. × intermedia: rounded shape. Cultivation as above. French lavender,
L. stoechas ♥: flowers have feathery bracts. Less hardy.

FRENCH LAVENDER
(*L. STOECHAS*)

DWARF WHITE LAVENDER
(*L. ANGUSTIFOLIA* 'NANA ALBA')

LOVAGE

Levisticum officinale
Lovage
This vigorous perennial bears flattened clusters of tiny yellow-green flowers in midsummer, followed by crescent-shaped seeds. A large plant, it needs plenty of space. Its bold foliage can make a handsome addition to the flower border.
Uses The leaves smell and taste strongly of yeast and celery, and can be used in salads and to flavour soups and other cooked dishes.

Young shoots can be eaten raw or steamed. The seeds are used in baking and for flavouring drinks. Preserve the leaves by freezing or drying, and the seeds by drying. The foliage may irritate some skins.
Cultivation Sow seed as soon as it ripens or in spring; divide in spring.
🔲 ◊ ✳✳✳

Lovage *see Levisticum*

Lungwort *see Pulmonaria*

M

Marjoram *see Origanum*

Meadowsweet
see Filipendula

Melissa officinalis
Lemon balm
A bushy, medium-sized perennial with lemon-scented leaves. The young foliage of golden-variegated 'Aurea' is particularly attractive in late spring and early summer.
Uses Fresh leaves give a delicate lemon flavour to salads, white fish dishes, and fruit desserts. Dried, they are used for herb teas and in pot-pourris.
Cultivation Cut plants back after flowering to produce plenty of fresh foliage. Variegated plants have a tendency to produce shoots that have reverted to plain green. Take these out at the base or they will eventually take over the plant. Divide in autumn or spring, or sow seed in spring; it may be slow to germinate.
🔲 ◊ ✳✳✳

MENTHA: Mint

Small to medium-sized perennials with creeping roots: generally invasive and best planted in a container sunk in the ground.

M. spicata
Spearmint
The most commonly grown. 'Crispa' has decoratively curled leaves; 'Moroccan' a particularly good flavour.
Uses Flavours potatoes, mint sauce and numerous dishes, especially Middle Eastern. Makes a refreshing tea. Medicinally, helps to relieve colds. Preserve by drying.
Cultivation All mints can be divided in spring or autumn.
⬛ ◊ ✻✻✻

M. × gracilis
Gingermint
Has a sweet scent. Yellow-and-green-leaved 'Variegata' looks attractive among other plants and is less invasive.
Uses Add to fruit salads.

M. × piperita
Peppermint
Uses Good in teas and iced drinks; can aid digestion.

M. requienii
Corsican mint
Tiny-leaved, creeping plant.
Uses Excellent for planting in paving cracks in shade.

GINGER-MINT

M. suaveolens 'Variegata'
Pineapple mint
Leaves are splashed cream.
Uses Add to fruit punches.

Monarda
Bergamot
Medium-sized, clump-forming perennial that brings colour and bees to the herb garden. The flowers, mainly pink, purple or red, appear in summer and autumn. The two main species are *M. didyma* (often called bee balm) and wild bergamot, *M. fistulosa*.
Uses Leaves of *M. didyma* are good added to iced drinks; they have a distinctive aroma similar to Earl Grey tea, flavoured with the bergamot orange. *M. fistulosa* is infused as a tea. Medicinally, bergamot is prescribed to ease digestive disorders. Preserve leaves and flowers by drying.
Cultivation Divide in spring. Sow seed in spring or autumn.
⬛ ◊ ✻✻✻

WILD BERGAMOT

Myrrhis odorata
Sweet cicely
A large, clump-forming perennial, with fern-like leaves and dainty clusters of small white flowers in spring, followed by long seed cases.
Uses The anise-flavoured leaves are used to sweeten fruit dishes; the seeds make an interesting ingredient in salads and fruit salads. Preserve leaves by freezing.
Cultivation Sow seed in spring, divide in autumn or spring. Plants will self-seed.
⬛⬛ ◊ ✻✻✻

Myrtus communis ♀
Myrtle
An aromatic evergreen shrub with small glossy leaves and fragrant cream flowers, single or double, in late summer. Grows slowly to a large plant.
Uses The leaves flavour pork and poultry dishes. The oil is used in perfumery, and the flowers dry well for pot-pourri.

DOUBLE-FLOWERED MYRTLE
(*M. COMMUNIS* 'FLORE PLENO')

Medicinally, myrtle is used to treat urinary and respiratory problems.
Cultivation Plant out of cold winds which scorch leaves. Suitable for containers but in cold areas may need moving into a greenhouse or conservatory for winter.
❏ ◊ ✷✷

N-O

Nasturtium *see*
Tropaeolum

Nepeta cataria
Catnip
Although there are several decorative, blue-flowered nepetas (catmint), such as *N.* × *faassenii*, this is the plant with magnetic appeal for cats. A medium-sized perennial, it has greyish leaves and white flowers in summer.
Uses Dried leaves can be used to flavour meat, infused to relieve colds – or put in mouse-shaped sachets for cats' toys.
Cultivation Divide in autumn or spring, sow seed in autumn.
❏ ◊ ✷✷✷

OCIMUM: Basil

Powerfully aromatic herb, much used in cooking, especially in Mediterranean and Southeast Asian cuisines. Generally grown as annuals, there are several different types; flavours vary among them.
O. basilicum
Sweet basil
Small, bushy plant with spikes of white flowers from summer to autumn. There are many to choose from: 'Mini Purpurascens Wellsweep' is particularly compact, with purple leaves and pink flowers; 'Green Ruffles' has huge, crinkled leaves and 'Horapha' (Thai basil) has a slight aniseed flavour. *O. basilicum* var. *minimum*, bush or Greek basil, is a small-leaved, compact plant that can be used as an edging to beds.
Uses Fresh leaves are delicious with tomatoes, pasta and in soup, and are used in Thai curries. Best preserved by freezing. Basil is used in aromatherapy.
Cultivation Needs sun

SWEET BASIL 'MINI PURPURASCENS WELLSWEEP'

and a sheltered site. Good results are achieved from growing in pots under glass or on a sunny windowsill or patio. Pinch out shoot tips to make plants bushy. Flavour coarsens once flowers form. Sow seed in late spring.
❏ ◊ ✷
Other basils
Holy basil, *O. tenuiflorum*: has downy leaves, which also taste slightly of mint. It is used in Thai cooking.

SWEET BASIL

SWEET BASIL
'GREEN RUFFLES'

Oenothera biennis
Evening primrose
A large, upright annual or biennial, ideal for informal herb gardens, especially if allowed to self-seed. Spikes of fragrant, pale yellow, bowl-shaped flowers open on summer evenings. They turn a darker gold as they age and are followed by downy pods containing tiny round seeds; the oil from these is rich in gamma-linoleic acid.

Uses The therapeutic qualities of this plant were only recently discovered; it is added to creams for dry skin and combined with other ingredients to relieve menstrual problems.
Cultivation Sow seed *in situ* from late summer to autumn. Can be grown in quite poor, stony ground.
❏ ◊ ✽✽✽

Onion *see Allium*

PELARGONIUM 'FAIR ELLEN'

ORIGANUM: Marjoram

Compact marjorams are ideal in pots and as edging; others suit mixed plantings. Some have variegated or gold foliage. White or lilac flowers appear in summer.
O. majorana
Sweet/knotted marjoram
Medium-sized annual.
Uses Good in tomato and onion dishes, especially of Mediterranean origin. Leaves and flowers can be used to make tea. Preserve by drying.
Cultivation Sow seed in autumn or spring.
❏ ◊ ✽✽

O. onites
Pot marjoram
Small, leafy perennial.
Uses Adds a more pungent flavour to food than sweet marjoram.
Cultivation As above, or take cuttings in late spring.
O. vulgare
Wild marjoram, oregano
Small hardy perennial. Gold-leaved 'Aureum' is best in light shade; 'Compactum' makes a neat edging.
Uses Flavours food, as sweet marjoram.
Cultivation As pot marjoram.

P

Parsley *see Petroselinum crispum*

Pelargonium
Scented pelargoniums
Grown for their aromatic leaves, scented pelargoniums look very different to the bold-flowered ones used as summer bedding. Most have small flowers in mauve, pink, purple or white, and are evergreen where protected from frost. Leaf shape and size varies, as does perfume, ranging from peppermint to rose, spice to eucalyptus. 'Fair Ellen' (*above*) has balsam-scented leaves.
Uses Dried leaves are excellent in pot-pourris. They can also be infused to flavour desserts and cakes; *P. crispum* 'Variegatum' ♀ adds a lemon taste. The essential oil, particularly of rose-scented 'Graveolens', is much used in perfumery and aromatherapy.
Cultivation In cold climates, best grown in pots to be moved indoors in winter. Cut

POT MARJORAM

WILD MARJORAM

FRENCH PARSLEY

back in spring to prevent plants from becoming leggy. Take cuttings in late spring or early summer.
🔲 ◊ Min 2°C

Petroselinum crispum
Parsley
This small, clump-forming biennial is one of the most widely used culinary herbs. Curly *P. crispum* has tightly crinkled leaves; the flat-leaved *P. crispum* var. *neapolitanum*, often called French or Italian parsley, has a stronger flavour.

CURLY-LEAVED PARSLEY

Uses Curly parsley has a clean taste and is best used fresh as a garnish or in salads. Flat-leaved parsley is stronger and is suited to cooked dishes. The flavour coarsens once flowers form. Preserve leaves by freezing.
Cultivation Sow seed in succession between spring and late summer. It can be slow and sparse to germinate.
🔲 ◊ ✱✱✱

Pot marigold *see Calendula*

Pulmonaria officinalis
Lungwort
A small, evergreen perennial with large, silver-spotted leaves, good for border edges and in wild or woodland settings where it can spread. The funnel-shaped flowers age gradually from pink to blue.
Uses Medicinally, lungwort was once used to treat bronchial diseases and is still prescribed as an expectorant.
Cultivation Cut back after flowering to encourage fresh foliage. Divide in autumn or after flowering.
🔲 ◊ ✱✱✱

R–S

Rocket *see Eruca*

Rosmarinus
Rosemary
This large, bushy, evergreen shrub looks very ornamental planted in mixed borders or against walls. Blue flowers (sometimes pink or white) open in spring. Some grow upright; choose low, spreading types for trailing over low walls or banks.

ROSEMARY
'PRIMLEY BLUE'

Uses The needle-like, aromatic leaves are good for flavouring meat, especially lamb and pork, and oils and vinegars. Rosemary is also used in bath preparations and shampoos. Preserve leaves by drying; they keep their flavour well.
Cultivation Cut back after flowering to prevent plants from becoming lanky. Avoid cutting into old wood. Plants can survive low temperatures better if drainage is good. Sow seed in spring.
🔲 ◊ ✱✱

ROSEMARY

FRENCH SORREL

Rumex
Sorrel
Medium-sized perennials grown for their acidic-tasting leaves. *R. acetosa*, common sorrel, is most widely used. The small, mat-forming *R. scutatus*, French or buckler-leaf sorrel, has a similar taste. Many relatives, including dock, are invasive weeds.

Uses Use leaves sparingly in salads, soups and sauces for fish. Harvest the leaves before plants form their spikes of tiny green flowers.
Cultivation Sow seed in spring, divide in autumn or spring.
❏ ◊ ✳✳✳

Ruta graveolens ♀
Rue
This small- to medium-sized, pungent-smelling shrub has attractive, finely divided, blue-green leaves. Yellow flowers appear in summer. There is a variegated rue with leaves splashed with cream.
Uses In homeopathy, rue is used as a remedy for sprains, bruising, eye problems and indigestion. Bitter-tasting, it has no culinary uses except as a flavouring for the Italian spirit *grappa*. Avoid contact with skin: in bright sunlight,

RUE

it can cause bad blistering.
Cultivation Will tolerate hot, dry sites. Sow seed in spring.
❏ ◊ ✳✳✳

St John's wort *see Hypericum*

Saffron *see Crocus*

SALVIA: Sage

A wide-ranging genus, most salvias are purely decorative, although the culinary sages also make extremely attractive garden plants.
S. officinalis
Common sage
The most widely cultivated for culinary use. A medium-sized shrubby perennial, with either grey-green or coloured foliage (*see right*).
Uses Leaves are mainly used to flavour meat. Preserve by drying.
Cultivation Cut back in spring to keep in shape. Sow seed in spring, take cuttings in spring or summer.
❏ ◊ ✳✳✳

Other species
Pineapple sage, *S. elegans* 'Scarlet Pineapple': large, scarlet-flowered. Leaves are used in fruit punches. Tender.

Clary sage, *S. sclarea*: open spires of cream, pink or lilac flowers are suitable for dried decorations. A medium-sized biennial or perennial.

GOLDEN SAGE ('ICTERINA')

PURPLE SAGE
(PURPURASCENS GROUP)

Sanguisorba minor
Salad burnet

A small, clump-forming perennial with attractively divided leaves and egg-shaped heads of tiny rust-coloured flowers in summer.

Uses The leaves have a cucumber scent when crushed, and can be added fresh to salads and summer drinks. Harvest before flowers open.

Cultivation Sow seed or divide in autumn or spring.

❏ ◊ ✿✿✿

Santolina chamaecyparissus
Cotton lavender

Tiny, yellow, button-like flowers decorate this small, round, evergreen shrub from mid-summer. These are held on long stems above the feathery grey-white leaves. Cotton lavender is often used as an edging in knot gardens.

Uses Dried leaves and flowers can be added to pot-pourris, or kept in cupboards to repel moths. Santolina was once used for skin irritations and against intestinal parasites; it is rarely used for medicinal purposes today. Preserve leaves and flowers by drying.

Cultivation Sow in autumn or spring, or take cuttings in early summer.

❏ ◊ ✿✿✿

Satureja
Savory

There are several types of savory. Summer savory, *S. hortensis*, is a small, bushy annual with narrow leaves and white or lilac flowers. Winter savory, *S. montana*, is a small, shrubby perennial with whitish-pink flowers. It can be used to edge beds, or grown at the front of a mixed

CREEPING SAVORY

border. The perennial thyme-leaved savory, *S. thymbra*, is also small and shrubby, with pink flowers. It, too, can be used as an edging. Creeping savory, *S. spicigera*, is a prostrate plant that looks good between paving stones.

Uses The leaves, especially of summer and winter savory, add a spicy, peppery flavour to meat and pulses. Preserve by drying.

Cultivation Give plants a light trim in spring. Sow seed in autumn or spring.

❏ ◊ ✿✿✿

WINTER SAVORY

Scented pelargonium *see Pelargonium*

Sorrel *see Rumex*

Sunflower *see Helianthus*

Sweet cicely *see Myrrhis*

Sweet woodruff *see Galium*

Symphytum
Comfrey

This large, vigorous perennial has coarse, hairy leaves and bears bell-like, pink, lilac, violet or pale yellow flowers in late spring and summer. Can be used as ground cover. Variegated comfrey will brighten shady corners.

Uses Comfrey leaves have a long history of use (fresh or dried) in poultices for bruises, sprains and abrasions. Taking internally is not recommended, as it contains alkaloids that, in large amounts, can cause liver damage. Contact with foliage may irritate skin.

Cultivation Sow seed in autumn or spring, divide in spring. Can be invasive.

❏ ◊ ✿✿✿

VARIEGATED COMFREY (*S.* × *UPLANDICUM* 'VARIEGATUM')

TANSY 'ISLA GOLD'

FEVERFEW

T

Tanacetum
Feverfew, tansy, alecost
With their daisy-like flowers and deeply cut leaves, it is worth including at least one kind of tanacetum in the herb garden. Feverfew, *T. parthenium*, is a small, bushy perennial, excellent for edging borders. Single or double flowers, white with a golden eye, appear above aromatic foliage in summer. 'Aureum' has golden leaves. Although short-lived, plants readily self-seed. Tansy, *T. vulgare*, is a medium-sized, spreading perennial, its upright stems topped with heads of bright yellow, button-like flowers in late summer. Alecost, *T. balsamita*, another medium-sized perennial, is less decorative. Small white daisy flowers appear in late summer and autumn above its mint-scented leaves.
Uses All can be added to pot-pourris. Medicinally, feverfew soothes insect bites and bruises, but can irritate some skins. Traditionally, it was used to relieve colds and fevers, but in recent clinical trials has been found to be successful in alleviating migraines. Fresh leaves may cause mouth ulcers if taken in quantity. Tansy leaves give a bitter, rosemary-like flavour to meat dishes and omelettes. Branches can be dried whole and used in cupboards to repel insects. Tansy oil is toxic and use of the herb is legally restricted in some countries. Alecost, once used to flavour beer, can be used sparingly in meat and vegetable dishes. Preserve leaves by drying.
Cultivation Sow seed in late winter or early spring, take cuttings in early summer, divide in spring or autumn. Feverfew and tansy can be invasive.
◻◻ ◊ ✤✤✤

Tarragon *see Artemisia*

Teucrium chamaedrys
Wall germander
This small, spreading perennial bears purple-pink flowers from summer to autumn. Evergreen leaves are small, with wavy edges. It makes a pretty edging for borders.
Uses Leaves are used to flavour liqueurs and vermouth. Medicinally, it is used for digestive disorders and as an appetite stimulant. It can cause liver damage, and is banned in some countries. Preserve leaves by drying.
Cultivation Divide in autumn, sow seed in autumn or spring.
◻ ◊ ✤✤✤

Tropaeolum majus
Nasturtium
An annual that can be small and bushy, or trail or climb. Funnel-shaped flowers in

WALL GERMANDER

THYMUS: Thyme

Thymes, all perennials, tend to make very small, shrubby plants, or creeping mats of aromatic foliage. They can be grown in cracks in paving and steps, to cover banks, in containers and rock gardens and in mixed borders and beds. Leaves can be gold or variegated silver or yellow. White, pink or purple flowers in summer attract bees.

🔲 ◊ ✳✳✳

T. serpyllum
Creeping or wild thyme
Mat-forming plant that can withstand being trodden on.
Uses Excellent in paving.
Cultivation Sow in spring, *in situ* if necessary.

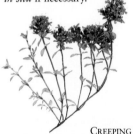

CREEPING
THYME 'RUSSETINGS'

LEMON THYME

T. vulgaris
Common/garden thyme
Mound-forming, shrubby plant. 'Silver Posie' has silver-variegated leaves.
Uses Flavours meat, poultry and game. Thyme oil is a powerful antiseptic. Preserve leaves by drying.
Cultivation Trim plants in spring, removing any dead stems. Sow seed in spring.
Other thymes
Lemon thyme, *T. × citriodorus*: small, bushy plant with lemon fragrance. 'Aurea' ♀ has golden leaves. Caraway thyme, *T. herba-barona*: creeping plant with caraway scent.

V–Z

Verbena officinalis
Vervain
A medium-sized, upright perennial with crinkled leaves and long, thin spikes of lilac or mauve flowers from mid- to late summer. Its rather straggly growth needs to be offset by placing it among large-leaved herbs for textural contrast.
Uses Vervain is taken for nervous disorders, and for minor injuries and skin problems. It tastes extremely bitter and has no culinary use. Preserve leaves by drying.
Cultivation Pinch out growing tips to encourage stems to branch. Sow seed in autumn or spring, or divide plants in spring.

🔲 ◊ ✳✳✳

Wall germander *see Teucrium*

Wild celery *see Apium*

Woad *see Isatis*

Wormwood *see Artemisia*

Yarrow *see Achillea*

vivid shades of red and yellow are borne from mid-summer to mid-autumn. The leaves of 'Empress of India' (*right*) are an attractive blue-green; those of 'Alaska' are splashed cream.
Uses Leaves and flowers add a peppery, cress-like flavour to salads, while the young, round seedpods are often pickled in vinegar and used like capers.
Cultivation Sow seed *in situ* in spring.

🔲 ◊ Min 3°C

NASTURTIUM 'EMPRESS OF INDIA'

INDEX

Page numbers in *italics* indicate illustrations.

ACKNOWLEDGMENTS

Picture research Mollie Gillard

Special photography Peter Anderson

Illustrations Gill Tomblin

Additional illustrations Karen Cochrane

Index Hilary Bird

Dorling Kindersley would like to thank:
All staff at the RHS, in particular Susanne
Mitchell, Karen Wilson and Barbara Haynes
at Vincent Square; Frank Hardy and Paul
Bearcroft, at Pershore and Hindlip College,
Worcestershire, for advice and technical
assistance; Candida Frith-Macdonald for
editorial assistance; Sarah Cleverdon for help
with planting designs; Rosemary Titterington
at Iden Croft Herbs, for advice and assistance;
Stanley Tools Ltd for tools and equipment.

The Royal Horticultural Society
To learn more about the work of the
Society, visit the RHS on the Internet at
www.rhs.org.uk. Information includes news of
events around the country, a horticultural
database, international plant registers, results
of plant trials and membership details.

Photography
The publisher would also like to thank the
following for their kind permission to
reproduce their photographs:
(key: t=top, b=below, l=left, r=right)

AKG London: Bibliothèque Nationale, Paris
8tr
Bridgeman Art Library, London/New York: *A
Garden*, by Johan Walter, French, *Florisège de
Nassau-Idstein* (1660), Bibliothèque
Nationale, Paris 8b
Eric Crichton Photos: 22b
E. T. Archive: British Museum 7br
Garden Picture Library: Jerry Pavia 40; John
Glover front cover c, 34; Juliette Wade 6
Garden Matters: 10cr
Jerry Harpur: RHS Chelsea designer:
Elizabeth Banks/*The Daily Telegraph* 5bc,
27br; designer Simon Hopkinson/Iden Croft,
Kent 12br
John Heseltine Archive: 2
Andrew Lawson: 15tl
Photos Horticultural: 11t; Michael and Lois
Warren 9b, 12b
Harry Smith Collection: 28
Steven Wooster: Chelsea Flower Show 5bl